End-to-End Web Testing with Cypress

Explore techniques for automated frontend web testing with Cypress and JavaScript

Waweru Mwaura

BIRMINGHAM—MUMBAI

End-to-End Web Testing with Cypress

Group Product Manager: Ashwin Nair

Publishing Product Manager: Pavan Ramchandani

Commissioning Editor: Pavan Ramchandani

Acquisition Editor: Nitin Nainani

Senior Editor: Sofi Rogers

Content Development Editor: Rakhi Patel

Technical Editor: Shubham Sharma

Copy Editor: Safis Editing

Project Coordinator: Kinjal Bari

Proofreader: Safis Editing

Indexer: Rekha Nair

Production Designer: Alishon Mendonca

First published: January 2021

Production reference: 1290121

Published by Packt Publishing Ltd.

Livery Place

35 Livery Street

Birmingham

B3 2PB, UK.

ISBN 978-1-83921-385-4

www.packt.com

To my wife, Irene, for her love, support, and inspiration

—Waweru Mwaura

Packt.com

Subscribe to our online digital library for full access to over 7,000 books and videos, as well as industry leading tools to help you plan your personal development and advance your career. For more information, please visit our website.

Why subscribe?

- Spend less time learning and more time coding with practical eBooks and Videos from over 4,000 industry professionals
- Improve your learning with Skill Plans built especially for you
- Get a free eBook or video every month
- Fully searchable for easy access to vital information
- Copy and paste, print, and bookmark content

Did you know that Packt offers eBook versions of every book published, with PDF and ePub files available? You can upgrade to the eBook version at packt.com and as a print book customer, you are entitled to a discount on the eBook copy. Get in touch with us at customercare@packtpub.com for more details.

At www.packt.com, you can also read a collection of free technical articles, sign up for a range of free newsletters, and receive exclusive discounts and offers on Packt books and eBooks.

Contributors

About the author

Waweru Mwaura is a software engineer with a specialization in automation testing and tools that make testing an interesting adventure and not just another item to cross off the software release list. He is an engineering hobbyist with interests ranging from hardware electronics and robotics to software development, architecture, and team development. Waweru is a lifelong learner and during his journey, he has helped organizations tackle testing problems and helped grow manual QA teams to automation teams with a focus on quality and defect prevention. In his free time, he practices professional photography.

I want to thank the people who have been close to me and supported me, especially my wife, Irene, and the amazing Packt team.

About the reviewers

Milena Paz is a software QA and automation engineer working with Cypress, from San Diego, California and currently residing in Miami, Florida. Her career began with the pursuit of a bachelor's degree in computer information systems and she has since worked with small and large technical organizations in the U.S. for a decade. She enjoys playing a key role in development teams and thrives in exceptionally fast-paced environments. She is always learning about and working with new and exciting tools for automation.

Vikas Kumar is an experienced technical test engineering leader with 13 years of experience in quality assurance, test engineering, automation, and release management. He is technically sophisticated with in-depth knowledge of tool development in UI, backend, mobile, and performance engineering. He has experience in building high-performing teams from the ground up, team management, software test engineering, the software life cycle, and automation concepts and frameworks.

He started his career in 2007, just after finishing his BE in electronics and communication from BITM, Bellary, and was campus-hired by HCL Technologies.

Vikas is currently residing in Abu Dhabi, UAE, with his wife and 5-year-old daughter. He loves driving, visiting new places, and spending time with family and friends. His hobbies are playing cricket, reading books, listening to music, and watching soccer – an ardent fan of FC Barcelona. In his free time, he also guides and mentors engineering college graduates and job seekers around software testing and automation frameworks.

Packt is searching for authors like you

If you're interested in becoming an author for Packt, please visit `authors.packtpub.com` and apply today. We have worked with thousands of developers and tech professionals, just like you, to help them share their insight with the global tech community. You can make a general application, apply for a specific hot topic that we are recruiting an author for, or submit your own idea.

Table of Contents

2

Differences between Selenium WebDriver and Cypress

3

Working with Cypress Command-Line Tools

4

Writing Your First Test

5

Debugging Cypress Tests

Section 2: Automated Tests with the TDD Approach

6

Writing Cypress Tests Using the TDD approach

7

Understanding Element Interaction in Cypress

8

Understanding Variables and Aliases in Cypress

9

Advanced Uses of Cypress Test Runner

Section 3: Automated Testing for Your Web Application

10

Exercise – Navigation and Network Requests

11
Exercise – Stubbing and Spying XHR Requests

12
Visual Testing in Cypress

Other Books You May Enjoy
Index

Preface

Cypress is a JavaScript automation testing framework created with the sole purpose of performing frontend testing. Cypress excels at re-inventing how testing is carried out, especially for the modern web. Unlike other testing frameworks, such as Selenium WebDriver, Cypress is much faster as it runs in the browser and also has a lower learning curve compared to other testing frameworks.

Developers working with frontend applications will be able to put their knowledge to use with this practical guide and develop their skills in end-to-end testing. This book takes a hands-on approach to implementation and associated methodologies that will have you up and running and productive in no time.

Who this book is for

The book is for testing professionals, software and web testers, and web developers who are well-versed in JavaScript and might or might not be familiar with the concepts of automation testing. The first three chapters offer a quick introductory guide that will help you familiarize yourself with how Cypress works and how to get started if you are a complete Cypress newbie. If you are a Selenium tester who wants to migrate to Cypress and uncover its capabilities, you'll find this book very useful. A good understanding of web testing and JavaScript is required.

What this book covers

Chapter 1, Installing and Setting Up Cypress, takes you through the essentials of getting started with Cypress, including the installation of the Cypress package, the default configurations, and the customization of settings. In this chapter, you will learn about how Cypress works, what modules it requires to run, the test file naming recommendations, and how to get started with using Cypress. Understanding how Cypress works will ensure that you are able to grasp the internal workings of Cypress and will be able to install and set up the subsequent projects on your own with a full understanding of the Cypress framework's structure.

Chapter 2, Differences between Selenium WebDriver and Cypress, is where we will explore how Cypress is different from the Selenium WebDriver and highlight some of the pros and the cons of choosing Cypress to run end-to-end tests. In this chapter, we will also explore elements that make Cypress more suitable to testing than Selenium and how users can extend its functionality.

Chapter 3, Working with Cypress Command-Line Tools, exposes you to the different Cypress commands that you can use to execute Cypress commands. The chapter will explain how to run the commands and also how to debug the application using Cypress commands.

Chapter 4, Writing Your First Test, will see you write your first test using Cypress. We will start with a passing test to check that everything works correctly, then move on to a failing test, and then we'll see how Cypress behaves and how the auto-reload feature works. In the second section of this chapter, we will focus on more advanced scenarios of getting you up to speed with how to properly write Cypress tests.

Chapter 5, Debugging Cypress Tests, dives into the different kinds of tools that Cypress includes to aid in debugging applications. Using Cypress' debugging tools, you will learn how to travel back to the snapshot of each command, see different page events that happened during execution, and visualize different commands and the times when elements were hidden and found. You will also learn how you can step forward and backward between command snapshots and pause and step through command snapshots in an iterative manner.

Chapter 6, Writing Cypress Tests Using TDD Approach, introduces you to **Test-Driven Development** (**TDD**) concepts and how you can apply them to writing Cypress tests. You will learn how to write tests using a TDD approach and also dive deep into how you can practically apply TDD in an application that is yet to be developed.

Chapter 7, Understanding Element Interaction in Cypress, covers how to interact with various elements of the DOM. The chapter will also teach you how to interact with animations, how to hover over elements, and how to check whether elements are disabled. By the end of this chapter, you will be comfortable with navigating through the DOM elements and writing meaningful tests for elements.

Chapter 8, Understanding Variables and Aliases in Cypress, explores how to deal with asynchronous commands through the use of aliases. We will also identify ways in which we can simplify our tests by using aliases. Finally, we will identify how to use aliases with routes and requests.

Chapter 9, Advanced Uses of Cypress Test Runner, looks at how to utilize the Cypress test runner to write better tests. Our focus will be on the instrument panel and the selector playground. We will learn how to use the instrument panel to understand the concepts of spying and stubbing and how Cypress interprets them.

Chapter 10, Exercise – Navigation and Network Requests, exposes you to practical examples and exercises aimed at practicing how to use and make navigation of network requests. The exercise will also combine concepts such as aliasing and use of variables to ensure that you are able to chain the different concepts learned about in the second section of the book.

Chapter 11, Exercise – Stubbing and Spying XHR Requests, looks at understanding what XHR requests are and how Cypress can assist in stubbing requests that take too long or that are complicated to receive responses from. Cypress stubbing will be important to ensuring that implemented tests are not flaky and that we can have custom responses instead of waiting for server responses from a request.

Chapter 12, Visual Testing in Cypress, covers how visual testing works in Cypress. We will explore what visual testing is, different types of testing, and how critical visual testing is to the modern web. We will also look at viewports and how they influence the process of visual testing and finally look at visual testing automated tools such as Applitools and Percy that we can use to carry out visual validation.

To get the most out of this book

You will need some understanding of JavaScript and you will need Node.js and the Yarn and npm package managers installed on your machine. All the code examples given have been tested on macOS and should work okay with all Linux OSes too. For Windows OSes, especially for the last three chapters, kindly read the additional notes in the callout box, in the *Technical requirements* section on how to run the commands on Windows. At the time of writing, all the examples have been tested with Cypress version 6.2.1.

Software/hardware covered in the book	OS requirements
Cypress 6.2	Windows 7 or above, macOS 10.9 (64-bit only) or above, or Linux (Fedora and Debian 8 (64-bit only))
Node.js	Windows, macOS X, or Linux
npm package manager	Version 5.2 or above
Yarn package manager	Version 2.0 or above

> **Important note**
>
> At the time of publication, this book was written with Cypress version 6.2.1, and some features may have been broken or deprecated. Kindly check our GitHub repository for the latest code updates and changes.

If you are using the digital version of this book, we advise you to type the code yourself or access the code via the GitHub repository (link available in the next section). Doing so will help you avoid any potential errors related to the copying and pasting of code.

Always try out the exercises; they are not just for fun but are crafted to help you learn and grasp the content of the chapters.

Download the example code files

You can download the example code files for this book from your account at `www.packt.com`. If you purchased this book elsewhere, you can visit `www.packtpub.com/support` and register to have the files emailed directly to you.

You can download the code files by following these steps:

1. Log in or register at `www.packt.com`.
2. Select the **Support** tab.
3. Click on **Code Downloads**.
4. Enter the name of the book in the **Search** box and follow the onscreen instructions.

Once the file is downloaded, please make sure that you unzip or extract the folder using the latest version of:

- WinRAR/7-Zip for Windows
- Zipeg/iZip/UnRarX for Mac
- 7-Zip/PeaZip for Linux

The code bundle for the book is also hosted on GitHub at `https://github.com/PacktPublishing/End-to-End-Web-Testing-with-Cypress`. In case there's an update to the code, it will be updated on the existing GitHub repository.

We also have other code bundles from our rich catalog of books and videos available at `https://github.com/PacktPublishing/`. Check them out!

Conventions used

There are a number of text conventions used throughout this book.

`Code in text`: Indicates code words in text, database table names, folder names, filenames, file extensions, pathnames, dummy URLs, user input, and Twitter handles. Here is an example: "The `cy.intercept()` command listens to XHR responses and knows when Cypress has returned a response for a specific XHR request."

A block of code is set as follows:

```
it('can wait for a comment response', () => {
    cy.request('https://jsonplaceholder.cypress.io/
comments/6')
    .as('sixthComment');
    cy.get('@sixthComment').should((response) => {
      expect(response.body.id).to.eq(6)
    });
  });
```

Any command-line input or output is written as follows:

```
npm run cypress:open
```

Bold: Indicates a new term, an important word, or words that you see onscreen. For example, words in menus or dialog boxes appear in the text like this. Here is an example: "To do this, open the browser console in your browser and click the **Network** tab, and then select the **XHR filter** option."

> **Tips or important notes**
> Appear like this.

Get in touch

Feedback from our readers is always welcome.

General feedback: If you have questions about any aspect of this book, mention the book title in the subject of your message and email us at `z`.

Errata: Although we have taken every care to ensure the accuracy of our content, mistakes do happen. If you have found a mistake in this book, we would be grateful if you would report this to us. Please visit www.packtpub.com/support/errata, selecting your book, clicking on the Errata Submission Form link, and entering the details.

Piracy: If you come across any illegal copies of our works in any form on the Internet, we would be grateful if you would provide us with the location address or website name. Please contact us at copyright@packt.com with a link to the material.

If you are interested in becoming an author: If there is a topic that you have expertise in and you are interested in either writing or contributing to a book, please visit authors.packtpub.com.

Reviews

Please leave a review. Once you have read and used this book, why not leave a review on the site that you purchased it from? Potential readers can then see and use your unbiased opinion to make purchase decisions, we at Packt can understand what you think about our products, and our authors can see your feedback on their book. Thank you!

For more information about Packt, please visit packt.com.

Section 1: Cypress as an End-to-End Testing Solution for Frontend Applications

This section focuses on the basic principles and development methodologies that we will use throughout the book. These introductory chapters are essential for understanding more about Cypress, how to set it up, and how it differs from other testing tools such as Selenium WebDriver.

We will first look at how to install and set up Cypress. Then, we will cover the different topics of Cypress' architecture and the differences between Cypress and Selenium. We'll then finally move on to writing our first test, where we will better understand how to properly debug Cypress tests.

In this section, we will cover the following chapters:

- *Chapter 1, Installing and Setting Up Cypress*
- *Chapter 2, Differences between Selenium WebDriver and Cypress*
- *Chapter 3, Working with Cypress Command-Line Tools*
- *Chapter 4, Writing Your First Test*
- *Chapter 5, Debugging Cypress Tests*

1 Installing and Setting Up Cypress

Cypress is an end-to-end test automation framework built and engineered for modern web applications. It focuses on eliminating inconsistencies in tests by ensuring that you can write, debug, and run tests on the browser without needing additional configuration or additional packages. Cypress works as a standalone application and can be installed on macOS, Unix/Linux, and Windows operating systems either using Hyphenate applications or command-line tools. Cypress was mainly built for developers who write their applications using JavaScript because it can be used to test all applications that run on a browser. In this chapter, we are going to cover the following topics:

- Installing Cypress on Windows
- Installing Cypress on macOS
- Installing Cypress via direct download
- Opening the Cypress test runner
- Switching Cypress browsers
- Adding npm scripts
- Running Cypress tests

By the end of this chapter, you will understand how to properly set up Cypress on both Windows and Mac operating systems and how to run Cypress tests. You will also understand how npm scripts can be used to automate the process of running tests and opening the test runner.

Technical requirements

Cypress can be installed as a standalone application on your computer and can be run on a machine that has at least 2 GB of RAM and that meets any of the following operating system requirements:

- macOS 10.9 and above (64-bit only)
- Linux Ubuntu 12.04 and above, Fedora 21, and Debian 8 (64-bit only)
- Windows 7 and above

In order to use Cypress on one of the operating systems listed here, Node.js 8 or above must be installed first. Node.js is a JavaScript runtime environment that allows JavaScript code to be run outside the browser. Installing Node.js installs npm, which allows us to install JavaScript packages from `https://www.npmjs.com/`. npm is the default package manager for Node.js, and users can either use it or use third-party package managers such as Yarn. In this section, we will install Cypress on both macOS and Windows operating systems.

Installing Cypress on Windows

In this section, we will install Cypress and Node.js on Windows operating systems so that we can run our tests.

Downloading and installing Node.js

The following steps will guide you through the installation of Node.js:

1. Visit the official Node.js website (`https://nodejs.org/en/download/`).
2. Select the Windows installer option.
3. Download the installer package.
4. Install the Node.js package by following the instructions on the Node.js website.

Next, let's initialize the project.

Initializing the project

As a best practice, Cypress is installed in the directory where the project is located; that way, we can be sure that the Cypress tests belong to the project. In our case, we will create a folder inside `Documents` and call it `cypress-tests`, then navigate to that directory when installing Cypress. We can use the following commands in a Windows PowerShell terminal to create the `cypress-tests` directory and navigate to it:

```
$ cd .\Documents
$ cd mkdir cypress-tests
```

After these commands are run successfully, we will then launch PowerShell and navigate to the directory that we just created with the following command:

```
$ cd .\Documents\cypress-tests
```

After creating the directory, we will then initialize an empty JavaScript project by running the following command in PowerShell:

```
$ npm init -y
```

This will create a default `package.json` file that will be used to define our project.

Installing Cypress on Windows

We will now install Cypress using npm in our project directory with the following command:

```
$ npm install cypress --save-dev
```

After running this command, you should be able to see the installation of Cypress and the installation's progress. This approach installs Cypress as a `dev` dependency for our empty project.

For the macOS installation, please refer to the next main section.

Recap – Installing Cypress on Windows

In this section, we learned how to install Cypress on the Windows operating system. We also learned how to use PowerShell to add Cypress to a project and also how to initialize an empty project. In the next section, we will look at how to install Cypress on macOS.

Installing Cypress on MacOS

In this section, I will be using a macOS machine to install both Cypress and Node.js. By the end of this section, you will have learned how to initialize an empty JavaScript project and also how to add the Cypress testing framework to macOS. We will also dive into how we can use either npm, Yarn, or direct Cypress downloads in our projects.

Installing Node.js

The following steps will guide you through the installation of Node.js:

1. Visit the official Node.js website (`https://nodejs.org/en/download/`).
2. Select the macOS installer option.
3. Download the installer package.
4. Install the Node.js package following the instructions on the Node.js website.

Next, let's initialize the project.

Initializing the project

To install Cypress, we need to navigate to the project folder and install it where we want the Cypress tests to be located. In our case, we will create a folder inside `Documents` and call it `cypress-tests`, then navigate to that directory when installing Cypress using our terminal. We will then launch our terminal application and navigate to the directory that we just created using the following command:

```
$ cd  ~/Documents/cypress-tests
```

After creating the directory, we will then initialize an empty JavaScript project by running the following command:

```
$ npm init -y
```

This will create a default `package.json` file that will be used to define our project.

Installing Cypress on Mac

To install Cypress, we will use the npm package manager that Node.js comes packaged with. To achieve this, we need to run the following command:

```
$ npm install cypress --save-dev
```

After running this command, you should be able to see the installation of Cypress in the `package.json` file and the installation progress on the command line. This approach installs Cypress as a `dev` dependency for our empty project.

For an alternative package manager that you can use with both Windows and macOS, you can use Yarn. We'll see how to install Cypress using Yarn in the next section.

Installing Cypress using Yarn

In both Windows and macOS, you can choose an alternative package manager. One of the available alternatives is the Yarn package manager. Just like npm, you first need to download the Yarn package manager using the macOS Homebrew package manager by running the following command:

```
$ brew install yarn
```

Just like npm, Yarn does the job of managing dependencies for your project and can be used as a project manager. An advantage that Yarn has over npm is that it is able to cache downloaded packages in such a way that it does not need to re-download the dependencies, therefore leading to better utilization of resources.

After the installation of Yarn, we can use it to install packages as we would with npm by running the following command:

```
$ yarn add cypress -dev
```

We have one final installation method, which is via direct download. This will be covered in the next section.

Installing Cypress via direct download

We can install Cypress for Windows, Linux, or macOS via direct download. This approach is recommended if you do not need to install the dependencies that come with Cypress or if you are only trying Cypress out. It is important to note that although this is the quickest way to install Cypress, this version does not come with features such as the ability to record tests to the dashboard.

The following steps will guide you through the installation of Cypress via direct download:

1. Navigate to `https://cypress.io`.
2. Select the **Download Now** link.

Cypress will automatically download as it will automatically detect the operating system of the user downloading the .zip file. You should then extract the zip file and run Cypress without installing any other dependencies.

Recap – Installing Cypress on macOS

In this section, we learned how to install the Cypress test framework on macOS using npm and also how to initialize an empty JavaScript project that will utilize the Cypress tests. We also learned how to use the Yarn package manager to install Cypress and how to directly download Cypress into our project without using any package managers. In the next section, we will look at how to open the Cypress test framework.

Opening Cypress

Installing Cypress is the first step on the journey of writing end-to-end tests; now, we need to learn how to use the tools that Cypress provides to run the tests using both the graphical user interface and the dashboards. There are four ways to run the Cypress executable that has been installed on your machine. After opening Cypress, you should then see the Cypress test runner. No matter which way you open Cypress, the test runner dashboard that you are presented with is the same. The following sections detail the different ways to open and run Cypress.

Running with Npx

npx is used to execute npm package binaries and comes with all npm versions from version 5.2. Npx can also be installed using npm from `npmjs.com`. To run Cypress using npx, you need to run the following command:

```
npx cypress open
```

Running with Yarn

If Cypress was installed using Yarn, you can then open Cypress using the following command:

```
Yarn run cypress open
```

Running with the node modules path

Cypress can also be run by referencing the root path of the installation on the node modules. This can either be by using the full path to the `node_modules` bin where the Cypress executable is located or by using the npm bin shortcut, as shown in the following sections.

Launching Cypress using the full path

This method of launching Cypress references the installed Cypress executable located in node_modules and works by running the executable to open Cypress:

```
$ ./node_modules/.bin/cypress open
```

Launching Cypress using the shortcut

Just like launching Cypress using the full path, this method launches Cypress in the same way but instead of referencing the full path, it uses the npm bin variable to locate the default location of the node_modules bin folder:

```
$(npm bin)/cypress open
```

Desktop application launch

If you downloaded your application as a desktop application, you can open Cypress by navigating to the location of the unzipped Cypress folder and clicking the Cypress executable that is present in the folder.

Now that we have successfully opened Cypress via our preferred method, we will look at how we can choose alternative browsers in Cypress if we do not wish to use the default browser that comes packaged with Cypress.

Recap – Opening Cypress

In this section, we learned how to open the Cypress test framework dashboard and also how to run Cypress in different ways, including running the Cypress dashboard using *npx*, *Yarn*, or with the *node_modules* path. In the next section, we will learn how to switch the browsers of tests running in Cypress.

Switching browsers

Cypress comes with Electron as the default browser on installation, but it can also integrate with other compatible browsers that contain the **Chromium project**, with the exception of Firefox. Currently, Cypress supports Firefox browsers Chrome browsers, Chromium, and Edge browsers. When launching Cypress, it will automatically find all the compatible browsers on the running machine and you will be able to switch between any of the browsers at any time using the test runner. To switch from one browser to another, you will need to click on the browser button at the top right and choose an alternative browser from the drop-down link.

Cypress tests can also be run or opened on different browsers using the command line, and this can be achieved by specifying the browser while opening the Cypress test runner or running the Cypress tests. All Chromium-based browsers, Edge, and Firefox can be launched using the command line with the following command:

```
$ cypress run --browser {browser-name}
```

The `browser-name` specified in the command can either be Edge, Chrome, or Firefox. To specify the path of the browser that Cypress should launch, you can choose to run the browser name with the executable binary of the browser instead of the name of the browser, as shown here:

```
$ cypress run --browser /path/to/binary/of/browser
```

Being able to switch browsers in Cypress ensures that a user can run their test suite on different devices and verify that the output from different browsers is consistent throughout the test suite. Switching browsers on Cypress also ensures that the verification of tests can take place and that all elements visible or actions that can be performed on one browser can be performed on another browser.

Let's use the knowledge we've gained so far to try out a practical exercise with Cypress.

Exercise

To combine the knowledge of opening Cypress and switching browsers, have a go at the following steps:

1. Navigate to the folder we created while initializing Cypress.
2. Run all the default tests that Cypress autogenerated when it was launched.
3. Switch the browsers on the test runner.
4. Rerun the tests with a different browser.

Now that we have learned how to run Cypress tests in different browsers, in the next section, we will explore how we can automate the process of running tests using npm scripts.

Recap – Switching browsers

In this section, we learned the different browsers that Cypress supports and how to switch different Cypress browsers either using the command line or using the Cypress dashboard. We also went through a simple exercise to help us understand how Cypress browser switching works and also how we run our tests using Cypress. In the next section, we will look at adding npm scripts to our `package.json` file to automate some of the Cypress tasks.

Adding npm scripts

`scripts` is a `package.json` property that gives a user the ability to run commands via the command line in JavaScript applications. npm scripts can be used to add environment variables to the properties of an application, package applications into production-ready bundles, run tests, or automate any other activity in JavaScript applications. npm scripts can either be used as defined by `npmjs.com` or customized based on the user's preferences and applications. In this section, we will learn how to write npm scripts to run our Cypress tests, to open our Cypress tests, and even to combine different npm scripts to achieve different results.

Opening a Cypress command script

To create a `scripts` command to open Cypress, you need to write the script name then add the command that npm will run when the script is executed. In this case, our command to open Cypress will be embedded in a script called `open`. We can achieve this by adding the following command to the `scripts` object in `package.json`:

```
"scripts": {
   "open": "npx cypress open"
 }
```

To run the `open` command, you simply need to run the `npm run open` command, and the test runner should open on the default browser selected in the Cypress test runner.

Recap – Adding npm scripts

In this section, we learned what npm scripts are and how to add them to the `package.json` file. We also learned how we can run the npm scripts that we have added to our `package.json` file to execute and automate tasks in our projects. Next, we'll learn how to run tests in Cypress.

Running Cypress tests

In this section, we will focus on how we can run Cypress tests on the browser. To do this, we will write test scripts that can run the tests similarly to opening Cypress scripts:

```
"scripts": {
"test:chrome": "cypress run -browser chrome",
"test:firefox": "cypress run -browser firefox"
}
```

The preceding scripts will be used to run tests either in the Chrome browser or in the Firefox browser depending on what command the user runs on their command-line terminal. To execute the tests, you can either run `npm run test:chrome` to run the tests in Chrome or `npm run test:firefox` to execute the tests in Firefox. The first section of the command instructs Cypress to run the tests in headless mode, while the second section instructs Cypress which browser to run the tests in. Running Cypress tests is not limited to only Chrome and Firefox and can be extended to any browsers that Cypress supports, with the option to customize the run script's name as you desire.

Combining Cypress commands using scripts

The `scripts` object in `package.json` gives you the flexibility to combine commands to create advanced commands that can carry out different functions, such as passing an environment variable to the tests being run, or even instructing Cypress to run different tests depending on the variable that has been passed. Combining Cypress commands ensures that we write short reusable statements that we can then use to construct a command that performs multiple functions when run. In the following example, we will use the `scripts` object to write a command to open Cypress, set the port, set the environment, and set the browser to either Chrome or Firefox depending on the command that we choose to run:

```
"scripts": {
"test": "cypress run",
"test:dev": "npm test --env=dev",
"test:uat": "npm test --env=uat",
"test:dev:chrome": "npm run test:dev -browser chrome",
"test:uat:chrome": " npm run test:uat -browser chrome",
"test:dev:firefox": "npm run test:dev -browser firefox",
"test:uat:firefox": "npm run test:uat -browser firefox"
}
```

The preceding scripts can run Cypress tests in two browsers. The scripts also assist in the identification of the environment to run the tests as specified by the `-env` variable. The last two scripts combine a series of scripts that run Cypress, attach an environment variable, and select the browser on which to run the tests, something that makes the scripts functionality of `package.json` very useful when it comes to writing Cypress commands to be executed in the test suite. To run the tests in Firefox, we simply run the `npm run test:uat:firefox` command for UAT or `test:dev:firefox` for the `dev` environment. You can also run Chrome tests with `test:uat:chrome` for UAT tests in Chrome and `test:dev:chrome` for the `dev` environment tests.

> **Important note**
>
> To run tests in different environments, you need to have configurations for running the tests in the different environments already set up in the project.

Recap – Running Cypress tests

In this section, we looked at how to execute our tests in Cypress. We also looked at different ways for our npm scripts to execute our tests by passing environment variables and changing parameters such as the browser in the scripts to run our tests. We also learned how to combine multiple Cypress commands to run our tests and therefore reduce the amount of code that we need to write.

Summary

In this chapter, we learned about installing Cypress both on Windows and on Mac operating systems. With both installations, we covered installing Cypress as a downloaded application or via the command line. We also covered using either the default package manager that comes with Node.js (npm) or third-party dependency managers such as Yarn. We learned how to utilize the test runner to run our tests and also how to automate our scripts in `package.json` to help us run our tests effectively. To test our knowledge, we also had an exercise where we practiced running tests in different Cypress browsers.

In the next chapter, we will be diving into the differences between Selenium and Cypress and why Cypress should be the preferred choice. We will be building further on the understanding of Cypress that we have gained in this chapter.

2
Differences between Selenium WebDriver and Cypress

Both Cypress and Selenium WebDriver are test automation frameworks that support end-to-end testing, and when someone mentions Cypress, there is a quick need to compare or find out which is better than the other. Before we get started on understanding the differences between Selenium WebDriver and Cypress, we will first need to understand the different motives for development between the two testing frameworks and who their intended users are.

Understanding the reasons why both Cypress and Selenium WebDriver are architecturally different will play a major role in helping you understand different and similar aspects of both the Selenium WebDriver and Cypress frameworks. In this section, we will evaluate ways in which both WebDriver and Cypress are unique, different, and similar in different ways.

We will explore the different use cases for both Selenium WebDriver and Cypress, and examine how each one is suitable for the purpose of its use. We will also clearly identify the audience of each of the testing frameworks, and what you can gain from both or each of them. We will describe why you should choose Cypress as a test automation framework and why it is a perfect candidate for end-to-end testing automation.

After understanding the differences and similarities between Cypress and WebDriver we will conclude by listing factors and tools that make it stand out and put it ahead of the curve when it comes to end-to-end web testing automation. The following are the key topics that we will cover in this chapter:

- Why choose Cypress?
- Comparing Cypress and Selenium WebDriver
- Using Cypress for frontend testing

By the end of this chapter, you will be able to understand the ways in which Cypress is different and similar to Selenium WebDriver and how it shows prowess in frontend web automation testing.

Why choose Cypress?

Cypress is an end-to-end testing framework that is written by developers, for developers and **Quality Assurance (QA)** engineers. Cypress focuses on testing web applications and since the only way to automate the web is by using JavaScript, Cypress only supports the use of JavaScript to write its tests.

Cypress was specifically written for frontend teams that utilize JavaScript for the development of their products, along with teams that need to quickly get started with the process of writing unit, integration, and end-to-end tests without the complicated intricacies of properly setting up a testing framework.

Cypress is not only beginner-friendly, but also ensures that everything that a developer or a QA engineer needs to get started on their tests is already packaged in the bundle that is downloaded and installed from the Cypress website. Cypress comes bundled with its own browser, a test runner, and chai as an assertion framework.

Having a bundle that contains everything required to get started with the process of writing tests means that anyone can just get started on the business of testing without needing to know about the setup process for assertion frameworks, test runners, or even the addition of browser drivers, such as in the case of using Selenium WebDriver.

Cypress makes use of JavaScript, which makes it significantly easier for JavaScript developers to onboard and quickly grasp the Cypress concepts. The ease of onboarding also ensures that developers and QA engineers can quickly get up to speed with writing tests using Cypress. Since Cypress is developed in JavaScript, developers and QA teams using JavaScript find it easier to debug and also understand the errors as they are similar to those in JavaScript applications.

Cypress utilizes a universal driver that is currently compatible with Firefox, Edge, Chrome, and the Chromium family of browsers. Unlike Selenium, which utilizes WebDriver and interacts with the **Document Object Model (DOM)** using HTTP network requests, the Cypress driver works directly in the browser without the need to make network requests. The ability to run inside the browser with the tests ensures that Cypress can effectively interpret commands without introducing timeouts when commands are passed from the tests to the driver and then to the application running in the browser.

Utilizing a universal driver also ensures that Cypress maintains the consistency of the methods that are utilized in all the browsers and also a standard format for the tests regardless of the browser that the tests will be run in. With this approach, it is possible for a QA team or an individual developer to grow their cross-browser testing as the only required thing is to run their existing test suites against the newly supported browser with Cypress.

The Cypress framework runs on the browser as it's architecturally different from any other test automation tools such as Selenium WebDriver. The ability of Cypress to run on the browser gives it a competitive advantage over other automation tools as it comes packaged with automatic wait sequences that could otherwise need to be defined in tests. Cypress therefore knows when to wait for an event, such as a network request, which would otherwise need to be specified as an explicit or implicit wait in a Selenium-driven test.

Software development technologies such as JavaScript frameworks change quickly than the testing technologies and frameworks that are available. Cypress presents a unique opportunity where the developers and QA engineers can quickly get started with the process of writing tests without the need to worry that a testing setup needs to be done. Removing the worry about the underlying test infrastructure not only quickens the testing process but also ensures that teams can quickly get started with the tasks that matter and are critical in the software development life cycle.

Recap – why choose Cypress?

In this section, we learned why Cypress is a preferred choice when it comes to web development testing and what makes it stand out from other test frameworks, including Selenium WebDriver. In the next section, we will be directly comparing the differences and similarities between Cypress and Selenium WebDriver.

Comparing Cypress and Selenium WebDriver

It is easy to fall into the trap of making assumptions that Cypress is a replacement for Selenium WebDriver and that its use could render Selenium WebDriver completely obsolete in the world of testing automation. While it is simple to directly assume that either Cypress is better or superior to Selenium or the other way round, this thinking is flawed and is incorrect in most instances.

In this section, we will cover why Cypress is unique and how its purpose is more complementary to Selenium WebDriver than supplementary. The following sections outline some of the differences between Selenium WebDriver and Cypress.

Browser driver

Cypress utilizes a custom universal driver for all the browsers that it supports, while on the other hand, Selenium WebDriver utilizes different drivers for each of the different browsers that it supports. The ability to use a universal driver for all the browsers means that on installation, we can run our tests on all the Cypress-supported browsers without the need to install an external driver. Selenium, on the other hand, requires a driver for every browser to be able to run tests in different browsers. The universal driver also gives Cypress a competitive edge as the team developing it is able to fix problems that are common in WebDriver, and can extend the functionality to different browsers.

Retries and waits

Cypress comes with built-in explicit retries to search for elements in the **DOM** and explicitly waits for events to happen before a test is considered to have failed. Cypress comes coupled with events that determine whether requests need to be waited for before the browser decides whether they have failed or passed. Cypress is able to handle the waits and retries because it runs on the browser with the tests and is able to understand the state of the tests at any given time.

Selenium, on the other hand, utilizes HTTP requests to WebDriver and it is therefore difficult for the framework to determine whether explicit or implicit waits are required when the tests are running. To solve the problem, Selenium users have to write the waits themselves in situations where the tests would need to wait for a request to complete before proceeding to the next step of execution. Selenium also does not come bundled with automatic retries when the tests are run, a feature that Cypress does possess.

Target usage

Cypress is built for JavaScript developers and QA engineers who want to quickly set up an automation framework and get to testing their end-to-end web applications, without spending too much bandwidth on setting up test frameworks or understanding the technologies behind building test frameworks. With Cypress, it is easy for developers to go beyond writing unit tests, to writing integration tests and even acceptance tests with features such as stubbing external dependencies, and testing how their applications behave. Cypress also currently favors developers and QA practices that are consistent with the Chromium family of browsers including Edge, with the addition of Firefox, which is currently in beta testing.

On the other hand, Selenium WebDriver is built to test anything that runs on the web. Selenium focuses on QA teams that want to test every aspect of their web applications and is not limited by factors such as browser compatibility or a single test runner, which is the case in Cypress. Selenium WebDriver gives the user options to extend it with different browsers and plugins, and also supports different languages such as Java, Python, Ruby, C#, JavaScript, Perl, and PHP. It is really difficult to plainly say that Selenium is a direct competitor to Cypress, as we can vividly see that while their use cases are closely similar, their audience and target users are totally different. While Selenium targets users of all major development languages, supporting even mobile automation in tools such as Appium, Cypress is only focused on making testing better for JavaScript web developers and QA engineers that understand the JavaScript language.

Architecture

Cypress runs on the browser and this gives it an edge over tools such as Selenium WebDriver. Running on the browser means that Cypress is significantly faster and can interpret commands quicker at runtime, as there are no third-party services interpreting the commands on its behalf or sending HTTP requests to the browser driver. While all the Cypress commands run inside the browser, it is possible for Cypress to tell what is happening outside the browser, as it has access to everything that the application has, including the window object, the DOM, a document object, or any other process and method. As long as your application has access, then Cypress tests will have access. The following diagram shows the architecture of Cypress versus the Selenium WebDriver architecture. Where in Cypress, the execution takes place in the browser, in Selenium, the execution takes place outside the browser:

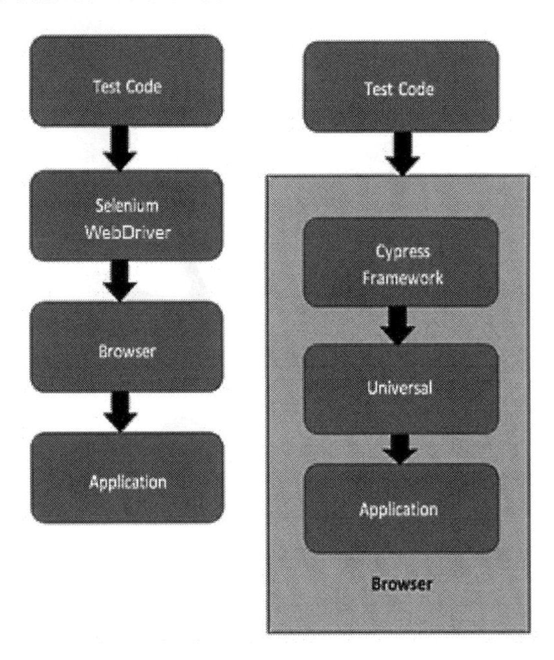

Figure 2.1 – Selenium versus the Cypress test execution architecture

Cross-browser compatibility

Cypress does not currently support all major browsers in the way Selenium WebDriver does. Cypress is currently supporting browsers built using the Chromium open source project, Firefox, Edge, and Electron (the default browser in Cypress). On the other hand, Selenium has support for all major browsers and this gives it an advantage when it comes to the ability to test applications on multiple platforms. While it is possible to argue that cross-browser functionality across more than three browsers increases the architecture complexity with minimal value to the testing process, support for multiple browsers may lead to identifying bugs that are of high priority, even though the severity of the bugs could potentially be low.

Cypress trade-offs

As mentioned previously, Cypress is a test automation tool that is focused on end-to-end test automation on the browser. Being able to run on the browser means that Cypress can interact with the elements on the browser better than any other tools but it also means that Cypress has permanent trade-offs that cannot be changed due to its architecture. The trade-offs are described in the following subsections.

Scope limitations

Cypress works best when used as an automation utility for QA engineers and developers who are writing tests. Cypress does not support tools for manual automation and has no plans to integrate manual testing tools in the framework.

Cypress is also not designed for activities such as web indexing and performance testing, and carrying out such activities may reduce the performance ability of the framework.

Environment limitations

Cypress runs on the browser and that means the language it supports will always be JavaScript, as the test code will always be evaluated in the browser. Being able to run in the browser means that to connect to a database or a server we can only use the Cypress commands of `cy.exec()`, `cy.request()`, or `cy.task()`, which provide a way to expose the database or the server, which might be more work than if we could explicitly define their configurations and Cypress understood them. Having tests run in the browser creates a great experience for running tests, but it is a little cumbersome to plug in functionality that needs to run outside the browser.

Multiple browsers and multiple tabs – limitations

The Cypress framework does not support the ability for a test to control multiple browsers when running. This is a permanent trade-off since the ability to control multiple browsers is not possible when running tests within one browser.

The Cypress framework does not support the ability to interact with more than one browser tab, as this functionality is not exposed inside the browser. However, Cypress provides the ability to incorporate other tools such as Selenium or Puppeteer to operate and drive multiple browser tabs when needed.

Control origin limitations

Cypress only supports visiting URLs that are from the same origin in the same test. The control origin limitation means that for any particular test, you are not able to visit different URLs that do not belong to the same origin. An example would be trying to send a request to `https://github.com` and `https://gitlab.com` in the same test, which would lead to an error. The following examples illustrate the improper and proper ways of utilizing the cross-origin when writing Cypress tests.

The proper way of utilizing cross-origin to run tests

In the following test, the user prompts Cypress to first navigate to the `https://github.com` GitHub website and then to `https://docs.github.com/en` (documentation link) for the GitHub resources. Both of the links belong to the same origin, `github.com`, and therefore Cypress would have no issue executing the requests:

```
It('can navigate to code repository hosting service', () => {
    cy.visit('https://github.com');
    cy.visit('https://docs.github.com');

  });
```

The improper way of utilizing cross-origin to run tests

In this test, the user prompts Cypress to first navigate to `https://github.com`, then later navigate to `https://gitlab.com`, which is of a different origin to the first URL. This will lead to an error being thrown when the test is run:

```
It('can navigate to code repository hosting service', () => {
    cy.visit('https://github.com');
    cy.visit('https://gitlab.com');

  })
```

Cypress and Selenium complementary actions

We can utilize both Cypress and Selenium together in some instances that are rare but still achievable when writing our tests. While Cypress has the limitation of not being able to control more than one browser tab, it is possible to configure Cypress to use Selenium to run multiple tabs. We can also utilize Cypress for our end-to-end tests and Selenium for activities such as load tests. Selenium has the ability to perform tests such as load tests, which are not supported in Cypress, and in such instances both test frameworks can be utilized together.

Summarizing the differences

Cypress is built for the web and is optimized to run on browsers. The architecture of Cypress allows it to effectively run tests, while at the same time overcoming the challenges of WebDriver. While Cypress is able to run on the browser, WebDriver interacts with the browser using the HTTP protocol, hence causing delays and unknown wait events when running tests. Cypress also targets QA engineers and developers who are looking to write tests without worrying about the underlying infrastructure and the limitation of one assertion library and programming language. Cypress also promises a future, as plans are underway to support Safari and Internet Explorer, that will ensure that developers and testers can try out Cypress on the browser of their choice.

With all the perks that Cypress comes bundled with, it also comes with some temporary and permanent trade-offs. Some of the temporary trade-offs are the ability to support all major browsers or to perform certain functions such as hovering over an element. The permanent trade-offs on the other hand mean that the architecture of Cypress cannot support them even in the future. They include aspects such as controlling multiple open browsers and/or operating multiple tabs in browsers, being able to connect to external databases and servers, and calling different cross-origins. All of the permanent trade-offs have workarounds and users can always implement the workarounds at will. Cypress, however, advises that workarounds should not be used in cases that would stretch Cypress beyond its intended purpose. Using Cypress for non-intended purposes may cause hurdles such as test automation complexity, which could end up reducing the effectiveness of Cypress as an automation tool.

Recap – comparing Cypress and Selenium WebDriver

In this section, we learned the advantages of using Cypress and also compared it to using Selenium to write tests. We also identified why Selenium is architecturally different from Cypress and why both are more complementary than they are supplementary.
We explored the trade-offs that Cypress has and some of the solutions to overcome the trade-offs that are permanent in the Cypress automation framework. In the next section, we will dive into the tools that make Cypress the best candidate for end-to-end web test automation.

Cypress for frontend applications

Cypress is built for the web, and that means it comes packed with some tools and features that other frameworks may not have. This improves the testing experience for frontend web developers and QA engineers. In this section, we will explore the different elements that Cypress is packed with that make it convenient and easy for its users to jump in and get started. The following are some of the elements that make Cypress stand out from other test automation frameworks for frontend applications.

Test Runner

The Cypress Test Runner comes by default when Cypress is installed on the user's machine. It is an interactive user interface that allows the user of the Cypress framework to see the commands that are running in the tests, and also the application that is under test as the commands interact with it. The Test Runner has the ability to show the number of test failures, test passes, skipped tests, the command log, and even the viewport of the browser when the tests are running.

Setup process

As explained in the previous chapter, the setup process of Cypress is not only clear and simple but it also ensures that the QA engineers and frontend developers need to run a single command to install Cypress. This eliminates the need to configure external dependencies to get started on the process of writing their tests. The Cypress documentation is also very interactive and clear, which makes it easy for developers and QA engineers to quickly onboard and use Cypress features.

Implementation and debugging

Cypress Test Runner comes with a built-in command log, and this means that when in **debug mode**, the user is able to check in real time the commands and assertions that have passed and the others that have failed. The ability to highlight failed commands and check which elements failed to be called, or what functions failed, is a capability that makes Cypress stand out, as debugging frontend applications not only becomes a walk in the park, but it also saves on the time that could have been used to investigate the cause of the failures. The command log also gives Cypress users instant feedback, and they can tell whether the tests have been properly written or not, just by checking the commands that are running on the Test Runner.

Exhaustive testing capabilities

Cypress combines the ability to write functional tests and also check responses from API calls made by the frontend. It also comes with visual regression capabilities that can identify whether an intentional change was made to the application under test.

When writing functional tests, the Cypress framework checks that the frontend functionality works as stipulated in the requirements document, and this would involve a process such as clicking a button or signing up a user.

API verification tests on the other hand check that the returned **XHR (XMLHttpRequest)** requests are successful with the correct responses received when the requests are returned. XHR requests provide an extra verification layer for API tests, as we can confirm that the structure of the expected data is similar to what we received in the frontend application.

> **Important note**
>
> XHR works as an API but is represented in the form of an object, and its main purpose is to transfer data between a given web server and a web browser.

Visual regression tests check the consistency of the elements in a page by comparing a page snapshot of the baseline to that of the latest test runs. If differences are spotted, then the tests being run will fail. On failure, a snapshot showing the differences between expected and generated images is created to show the differences between the generated snapshot and the baseline image. After a test run, the QA engineer or developer can then accept or reject the changes that have been made to the frontend application in relation to the application changes.

Recap – Cypress for frontend applications

In this section, we learned why Cypress is the most suitable when it comes to testing frontend applications. We learned of different elements that make it a preferable testing framework and the way that we can leverage its strengths to write better and more exhaustive tests.

Summary

It is without a doubt that Cypress is a powerful tool that can be leveraged by frontend teams and QA engineers to quickly get started and write tests without worrying about the overhead that comes with building test automation tools from the ground up. In this chapter, we learned why Cypress is the best web automation framework for testing, and we did this by comparing the different tools between Cypress and existing test automation tools. We also covered the differences between Cypress and Selenium, and the specific architectural similarities and differences between the two. Finally, we explored how we can leverage the tools. In the next chapter, we will learn how to use command-line tools to run, test, and debug Cypress tests.

3
Working with Cypress Command-Line Tools

In the previous chapter, we learned how Cypress differs from other test automation tools such as Selenium and how it stands out when it comes to web automation testing. In this chapter, we will build on our knowledge of using Cypress using command-line tools. To do this, we will cover commands that you can use to make use of Cypress' functionality.

Some of the commands will involve functions such as running individual or all tests, debugging Cypress, and launching Cypress tests on different browsers, among other Cypress command-line functions. We will be referencing the GitHub repository folder for this chapter, and every command and piece of code that will be written will be included in the repository for your reference and practice.

We will cover the following key topics in this chapter:

- Running Cypress commands
- Understanding basic Cypress commands
- Cypress debugging on the command line

Once you've worked through each of these topics, you will be ready to write your first test.

Technical requirements

The GitHub repository for this chapter can be found at `https://github.com/PacktPublishing/End-to-End-Web-Testing-with-Cypress`.

The source code for this chapter can be found in the `chapter-03` directory.

To run the examples in this chapter, you will need to clone this book's GitHub repository and follow the `READMe.md` file's instructions on how to properly set up and run the tests. You can read more about how to use GitHub to clone projects on your local machine at `https://docs.github.com/en/free-pro-team@latest/github/creating-cloning-and-archiving-repositories/cloning-a-repository`.

Running Cypress commands

Effective utilization of the Cypress framework requires you to have an understanding of Cypress and how different functionalities can be run using the command line. Cypress commands allow the users of the Cypress framework to automate processes, and also to provide specific instructions to the framework and to the tests during initialization and runtime.

In most instances, running Cypress tests through the command line is quicker than running them using the browser. This is because running tests through the command line reduces the number of resources required to run a specific test. The reason for this is that tests that run in the command line are normally headless, which means less resources are allocated to run the tests, which is not the same for test execution in headed mode.

> **Important note**
>
> Headed mode is when tests can be visually seen running on a browser, while in headless mode, the test execution process does not open a visible browser. Instead, all the tests are run and output on the command line.

First, let's look at how to run global and local Cypress commands.

Global and local commands

Cypress commands can either be run from a specific directory containing a Cypress installation and code, or run from the global Cypress installation. Globally installing Cypress ensures that users can run Cypress from any directory in the operating system, while with a local Cypress installation, Cypress can only be accessed from the single directory that it has been installed in.

Running global Cypress commands

Global commands in Cypress are run by accessing the globally installed version of Cypress. The commands that are invoked when running the global version of Cypress are not necessarily generated or defined by the user since they are built into the framework. To be able to run Cypress commands globally, you need to install Cypress globally with the following command:

```
npm install cypress --global
or (shorter version)
npm i -g cypress
```

The preceding command will install Cypress globally and ensure that invoking any known Cypress command from any Cypress installation directory will yield a result or an error, depending on the execution of the provided command.

To run a global command, you need to define the command using the `cypress` keyword, then the command; for example, `cypress run` or `cypress open`.

Running local Cypress commands

Local Cypress commands are derived from Cypress global commands and are an alternative to running commands globally. To run Cypress commands locally, you will need to install Cypress in your directory with the following command:

```
npm install cypress
or (shorter version)
npm i cypress
```

We can integrate the required commands into the development environment by defining them in the `package.json` file, under the `scripts` section, as shown here:

```
{
  "scripts": {
    "cypress:run": "cypress run",
```

```
        "cypress:open": "cypress open"
    }
}
```

Adding commands to `package.json` allows us to use these commands in the same way we would execute npm commands for JavaScript packages. The commands defined in the `package.json` file are interpreted by the Node.js environment at runtime and when executed, they are executed as if the commands are global commands.

> **Important note**
>
> It is recommended that you run the `npm init` command in a Terminal before running the `npm install cypress` command. If Cypress is run without a project being initialized, Cypress' directories will not be visible. By running the `init` command, cypress recognizes the project directory as an existing project, so it initializes and creates its directories without us needing to run additional commands on the Terminal.

Defining commands in `package.json` not only makes it easier for developers and QA engineers to know which commands to run, but it also simplifies the nature of the commands that a person needs to run when running, debugging, or maintaining their tests.

> **Important note**
>
> The Cypress development team recommends installing Cypress per project and not using the global installation approach. The local installation provides certain advantages, such as users having the ability to quickly update the Cypress dependency and reducing the Cyclic dependency problems that would break some tests in a different project, while Cypress runs fine in another project.

To run scripts in the command line, you need to invoke `npm run`, followed by the command's name. In the commands we defined previously, you would simply need to run the following to execute the commands simultaneously:

```
npm run cypress:run  // command  to run tests on terminal
npm run cypress:open // command to run tests on cypress runner
```

Time for a quick recap.

Recap – running Cypress commands

In this section, we learned how to invoke either local or global commands, as well as how to run tests from the Cypress Terminal or the test runner, which utilizes a graphical user interface. In the next section, we build on the knowledge we have garnered of running Cypress commands to understand how different commands are utilized within Cypress.

Understanding basic Cypress commands

In this section, we will explore various Cypress commands that we can use to run our tests either via the Terminal or using the Cypress test runner. We will also observe how the commands can be used to achieve different results. This section will also introduce us to customizing different tests that interact with our applications to achieve specific results. We will dive into the most common Cypress commands and how they can be extended with options that come pre-built into the Cypress framework. The commands we will explore are as follows:

- `cypress run`
- `cypress open`
- `cypress info`
- `cypress version`

Let's start with `cypress run`.

cypress run

The `cypress run` command executes all the tests in a Cypress suite in a headless manner, and runs the tests in the Electron browser by default. If it's not extended with any other configurations, the command will run all the files in `.spec.js` format in the `integration` folder of Cypress. The `Cypress run` commands can be run with the following configuration options:

```
cypress run {configuration-options}
```

The most common Cypress configuration options include the following:

`--env or -e`	Used as an option to define an environment variable through the command line at runtime.
`--browser or -b`	Specifies the browser that the test will run in.
`--config or -c`	Defines a configuration such as the timeout period when the test is running. This value overrides the value in `cypress.json` if the same key-value pair has been declared.
`--config-file or -C`	Specifies the configuration file used to run the tests. The values declared in this file override the ones in the `cypress.json` file.
`--headed`	Runs the tests after launching a browser.
`--headless`	Runs the tests without launching a browser.
`--spec` or `-s`	Specifies the `spec` files to be run.

The next few sections will expand on each configuration option shown in the preceding table.

cypress run --env <env-variable>

Cypress environment variables are *dynamic name-value pairs* that influence the way Cypress executes tests. These environment variables are useful when there is a need to run the tests in multiple environments, or when the values defined are prone to quickly changing.

In Cypress, you can define single or multiple environment variables either as strings or JSON objects.

In this section, we will write tests for an open source **todoMVC** application. The code base for these tests can be found in the `chapter 03` directory, in the GitHub repository for this book. The application under test is a **To-do list** application that's been developed in React. Using the application, we can add our todo items, mark them as completed, delete them, view completed items, and even toggle between the *active*, *all*, and *completed* todo items.

Using this application, we may have plans to extend the application to serve a secure version of the application using **HTTPS** instead of the current **HTTP** protocol. Even though the functionality for HTTPS is not currently supported, we can add provisions for it using our environment variables in the Cypress tests. To achieve this, we will define the **Transfer protocol** URL portion as an environment variable, then pass this to our commands in `package.json`, as shown in the following examples.

The following code snippets can be found in the GitHub repository mentioned in the subfolder in `chapter 03`. The full source code for the `Todo-app.spec.js` file is located under the `Cypress/integration/examples` folder. The Cypress tests we will be exploring in this chapter are the version 1 tests.

The following `Todo-app.spec.js` file demonstrates how to use environment variables when navigating to a URL. It is the main test file and is located in `chapter-03/cypress/integration/examples/todo-app.spec.js` in this book's GitHub repository:

```
...
context('TODO MVC Application Tests', () => {
  beforeEach(() => {
    cy.visit(
      `${Cypress.env('TransferProtocol')}://todomvc.com/
examples/react/#/`)
  });
...
```

The following `package.json` file is also located in the `chapter-03/` directory and holds all the commands that are used to execute the testing or execution commands of the JavaScript application. It is located in the root location of the `chapter-03/` directory:

```
...
"scripts": {
    "cypress:run": "cypress run --env
    TransferProtocol='http'",
    "cypress:run:v2": "cypress run --env
    TransferProtocol='https'",
  },
...
```

The preceding script demonstrates that in the event of a change occurring in the URL protocol, we can run any of the aforementioned test commands to replace the environment variable we declared in the URL when we are running our Cypress tests. We can execute the preceding scripts with `npm run cypress:run` and `npm run cypress:run:v2` consecutively.

> **Important note**
>
> HTTPS is the same as HTTP, with the difference being that HTTPS is more secure. This is because the process of sending requests and receiving responses is encrypted using the TLS(SSL) security protocol.
>
> The transfer protocol is the portion of the URL that determines whether the URL uses the HTTP or HTTPS protocol. A URL using the HTTP protocol begins with `http://`, while one that uses HTTPS begins with `https://`.

cypress run --browser <browser-name>

The Cypress command line has the built-in capability to run Cypress tests in different browsers that have been installed on the host computer, and that are supported by the Cypress framework. Cypress tries to automatically detect the installed browsers and can run the tests in either `chrome`, `chromium`, `edge`, `firefox`, or `electron`. To run tests in a specific browser, you will need to supply the browser name using the `--browser` configuration option. You can also choose to supply the browser path instead of the browser name; Cypress will still run the tests in the supplied browser path, as long as it is valid and supported by Cypress.

The following code snippet shows scripts that have been defined in the `scripts` section of `package.json` in the `chapter-03` directory of this book's GitHub repository. The scripts define the browsers that our tests will run in and also pass in an environment variable for a part of the URL:

```
...
"scripts": {
    "cypress:chrome": "cypress run --env
    TransferProtocol='http' --browser chrome",
    "cypress:firefox": " cypress run --env
    TransferProtocol='http' --browser firefox"
  },
...
```

In the preceding commands, we can run our tests in either Chrome or Firefox using the `npm run cypress:chrome` and `npm run cypress:firefox` commands, respectively.

> **Important note**
>
> To run tests in a specific browser, the browser must be installed on your machine and it must also be among the list of Cypress supported browsers.

Cypress run --config <configuration(s)-option>

Cypress can set and override configurations using commands running on the terminal. Cypress' configuration can either be passed as a single value, as multiple values separated by commas, or as a stringified JSON object. Any defined configuration in Cypress can be changed or modified by the `cypress run --config` configuration option. Configuration options may include specifying an alternative `viewportHeight` and `ViewportWidth`, timeouts, and file changes, among other configurations. In our script, we will change the viewport that Cypress runs our tests on, and instead of the default viewport, which is 1000x660, we will run our tests in the tablet viewport of 763x700.

The following code snippet is defined in the `package.json` file of our `chapter-03` root directory. The following script is used to run tests in a tablet viewport. To do this, you must override the Cypress default configuration for the viewport's height and width:

```
...
"scripts": {
"cypress:tablet-view": "cypress run
--env TransferProtocol='http' --config
viewportHeight=763,viewportWidth=700",
}
...
```

The previous script can be run with the `npm run cypress:tablet-view` command.

> **Important Note**
>
> When passing more than one configuration option in Cypress, leave no spaces between the comma-separated values for the different configurations (as shown in the preceding code); otherwise, Cypress will throw an error.

cypress run --config-file <configuration-file>

Cypress can override the default configuration file located at `/cypressRootDirectory/cypress.json`. You can define one or more secondary Cypress configuration files in order to run their tests. Cypress also allows you to entirely disable the use of a configuration file.

The following script, which is located in `package.json` in the root directory of our `chapter-03` directory, is a command that enables Cypress to override the configuration file that it uses to run the tests. When the command is executed, rather than using the default `cypress.json` file located in `chapter-03`, it will use the `cypress-config.json` file, which is located under `chapter-03/config/cypress-config.json`:

```
...
"scripts": {
"cypress:run:secondary-configuraton": "cypress run --env
TransferProtocol='http' --browser chrome --config-file config/
cypress-config.json"
},
...
```

To run the preceding script, you will need to run the `npm run cypress:run:secondary-configuraton` command, which will run the tests with the configuration file located at `/cypressRootDirectory/config/cypress-config.json`.

cypress run --headed

Cypress provides a command that allows you to run browsers in both headless and headed mode. When headed mode is defined, the tests open a browser when they are run. This option can be used in the default Electron browser that Cypress comes bundled with. The default mode for running Cypress tests using the `run` command in Electron is headless, and to override this, we need to pass the `--headed` configuration when the tests are running.

The following script can be found in the `package.json` file, which is located in the `chapter-03` directory of this book's GitHub repository. Running the following script command will enable Cypress to be run in headed mode, which allows tests being run to be visible on the browser:

```
...
"scripts": {
"cypress:electron:headed": "cypress run --env
TransferProtocol='http' --headed"
},
...
```

The previous script can be run with the `npm run cypress:electron:headed` command.

cypress run --headless

Cypress runs tests in both Chrome and Firefox browsers in headed mode, and this launches a browser every time the tests are run. To change this behavior and ensure that test runs occur without launching a browser, you need to configure the commands running either the Chrome or Firefox browser so that they run headlessly.

The following script can be found in the `package.json` file, which is located in the `chapter-03` directory of this book's GitHub repository. Running the following command will enable Cypress to run in headless mode, where the test commands can only be seen running on the command-line interface:

```
...
"scripts": {
"cypress:chrome:headless": "cypress run --env
TransferProtocol='http' --browser chrome --headless",

"cypress:firefox:headless": "cypress run --env
TransferProtocol='http' --browser firefox --headless"
},
...
```

To run Chrome in headless mode using the preceding commands, you will need to run `npm run cypress:chrome:headless`. To run the commands in headless mode in Firefox, you will need to run the `npm run cypress:firefox:headless` command.

cypress run --spec <spec-file>

Cypress allows us to specify the different test files that can be run. With this command, it is possible to specify a *single* test file to be run in a directory, instead of running *all* the test files in a directory. It is also possible to specify different tests in different directories so that they run simultaneously, and to specify a regex pattern that matches a specific directory.

The following code snippet is part of the `package.json` file, which is located in the `chapter-03` directory of this book's GitHub repository. The first script can only run a specific file in a directory, while the second script can run multiple files within a single directory:

```
...
"scripts": {
  "cypress:integration-v2:todo-app": "cypress run --env
  TransferProtocol='http' --spec 'cypress/integration/
```

```
    integration-v2/todo-app.spec.js'",
    "cypress:integration-v2": "cypress run --env
    TransferProtocol='http' --spec 'cypress/
    integration/integration-v2/**/'"
  },
...
```

The first command specifies that the test will run the `todo-app.spec.js` file, which is located in the `integration-v2` folder. The second command will run all the test files that are located in the `integration-v2` folder.

cypress open

The `cypress open` command runs Cypress tests in a test runner, with the configuration options being applied to the tests of the project that you are running. The configuration options that are passed when you're running the `cypress open` command also override the specified defaults in the `cypress.json` file, which is located in the `tests root` folder, if configurations are specified when the tests are running. The following command shows how to run any `cypress open` commands:

```
cypress open {configuration-options}
```

The first part of the command shows the `cypress open` command, while the second part shows the configuration options that can be chained with it.

The most common Cypress configuration options include the following:

`--env` or `-e`	Used as an option to define environment variables.
`--browser` or `-b`	Specifies custom browser paths.
`--config` or `-c`	Defines a configuration, such as the timeout period when the test is running. This value overrides the value in `cypress.json` if the same key-value pair has been declared.
`--config-file` or `-C`	Specifies the configuration file that will be used to run the tests. The values declared in this file override the ones in the `cypress.json` file.
`--global`	Runs the tests in global mode.
`--project`	The project path of the tests to be run.
`--port`	Specifies the port to run the Cypress tests on.

We will look at each option in detail in the next few sections.

cypress open --env <env-variable(s)>

Just like running the `cypress run` commands, the `cypress open` command can be run with specified environment variables that are declared when the tests are running. Similar to the `cypress run` command, it is possible to declare one or multiple environment variables using the `--env` configuration option when running the tests in the test runner.

In the previous section, we specified how we can run tests via the command line by passing an environment variable in the `cypress run` command. We will pass the same environment variable to run the tests using our Cypress test runner, and the tests should run okay. The environment variable that's passed will determine whether the transfer protocol of the **todoMVC** application URL is **HTTP** or the secure **HTTPS**.

The following code snippet is located in the `Todo-app.spec.js` file, which is the main test file in our `chapter-03/` directory. The `todo-app.spec.js` file can be found under `integration/examples` in the `chapter-03/` directory. In the following snippet, just like in `cypress run`, we can pass environment variables to the URL using the `cypress open` command:

```
...
context('TODO MVC Application Tests', () => {
  beforeEach(() => {
    cy.visit(
      `${Cypress.env('TransferProtocol')}://todomvc.com/
examples/react/#/`)
  });
...
```

The following code snippet is located in the `chapter-03/` root directory in the `package.json` file. Using this snippet, we pass the `'http'` environment variable to our tests. This is when we can complete our URL and execute our tests:

```
...
"scripts": {
    "cypress:open": "cypress open --env
    TransferProtocol='http'"
  },
...
```

To open the test runner and verify that the tests run, you can run `npm run cypress:open`, which should automatically add the **TransferProtocol** environment variable to the running tests' configuration.

cypress open --browser </path/to/browser>

When specified, the `--browser` option points to a custom browser that will be added to the list of available browsers in the test runner. The browser to be added must be supported by Cypress and must be installed on the machine that is running the Cypress tests.

By default, all the available browsers can be viewed in Cypress by clicking on the browser selection button in the test runner, before selecting the spec to run. The browser selection dropdown contains all the browsers that have been installed on the system and are supported by Cypress. The browser selection dropdown also allows you to switch the test browsers, and therefore test the functionality under different browsers:

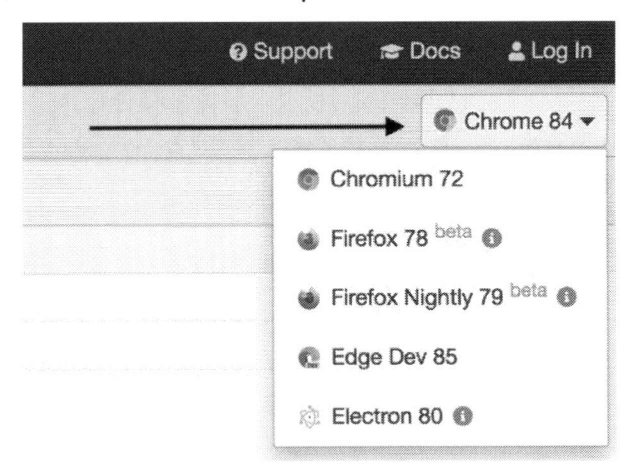

Figure 3.1 – Test browser selection dropdown

To specify a path so that the browser can be added (for example, Chromium), you need to have the following configuration to add Chromium to the list of available browsers. Here, you need to run the `npm run cypress:chromium` command.

The following script is located in the `chapter-03/` directory under the `package.json` file in this book's GitHub repository. When the script is executed as a command, it will look for a browser in the specified location and add it to the list of browsers used to run the Cypress tests:

```
...
"scripts": {
```

```
        "cypress:chromium": "cypress open --browser
        /usr/bin/chromium"
    },
..
```

To execute the preceding script to run our tests, we need to run the `npm run cypress:chromium` command in our Terminal. This will locate the Chromium browser in the `location /usr/bin/chromium` and use it to run our tests.

cypress open --config <configuration-option(s)>

The Cypress framework allows us to run tests in a test runner and provide configuration options that must be passed when initializing the test runner. While passing the `--config` option, it is possible to either pass one environment variable or multiple environment variables that are separated by commas. The following script specifies that the viewport dimensions should be for a tablet and that the configurations are passed through the `-config` option. To run the required command, you need to run `npm run cypress:open:tablet-view`.

The following script, located in the `package.json` file in this book's `chapter-03/` root directory, is used to change the configuration of the viewport for a test running on the visible browser:

```
...
"scripts": {
        "cypress:open:tablet-view":"cypress open --env
        TransferProtocol='http' --config
        viewportHeight=763,viewportWidth=700"
    },
...
```

When executed, the command modifies the default Cypress configuration for the browser's size. The provided viewport height and viewport width will show content in a similar fashion to a tablet display.

> **Important note**
>
> The configuration options specified using the `--config` option will overwrite the default configuration specified in the `cypress.json` file.

cypress open --config-file <configuration-file>

Just like in the case of the `Cypress run` command, Cypress tests running through the test runner can have an override configuration file that overrides the default `cypress.json` file, which contains the default Cypress configuration. It is located in the root folder of the test file.

The following code snippet, located in the root folder of the `chapter-03/` directory's `package.json` file, overrides the default Cypress configuration file, which is identified as `cypress.json`. When executed, the command will read an alternative configuration file that has already been declared in `chapter-03/config/cpress-config.json`:

```
...
"scripts": {
"cypress:open:secondary-configuraton": "cypress open --env
TransferProtocol='http' --config-file config/cypress-config.
json"
},
...
```

To execute the previous command and change the default Cypress configuration file's location, you need to run the following command in your command-line interface:

```
npm run cypress:open:secondary-configuration
```

Now, let's look at another command.

cypress open --global

As we mentioned earlier, Cypress can be installed globally. Instead of installing it in every project, you can use the global Cypress installation to run different Cypress tests. This global installation also allows you to trigger global commands without necessarily having an installation of Cypress in the specific directory where the Cypress commands are invoked. To open Cypress in global mode, you need to pass in the `--global` option, as shown here:

```
cypress open --global
```

By running this command, Cypress will recognize that we want to execute the tests using the global version of Cypress, not our local instance.

cypress open --project <project-path>

Cypress comes with the built-in capability to override the default path that Cypress starts when running the tests. When the `--project` option is defined, it instructs Cypress to abandon the default directory/project path, and instead use the provided project path to run the Cypress tests that are located in the specified project path. In this setup, it is possible to run totally different Cypress projects located in different directories or nested directories.

The following code snippet, located in the `package.json` file of this book's `chapter-03/` root directory, executes tests in a totally different Cypress project. The script executes a project located in `chapter-03/cypress/todo-app-v3`:

```
"scripts": {
"cypress:project:v3": "cypress open --env
TransferProtocol='http' --project 'cypress/todo-app-v3/'"
},
```

In the previous script, a user can run a different Cypress project located in the `cypress/todo-app-v3` folder. To run the script, we need to run the `npm run:cypress:project:v3` command. The `version-3` project is a standalone project that does not depend on the parent Cypress project. It can use its `cypress.json` file to determine its run configurations, as shown in the following screenshot:

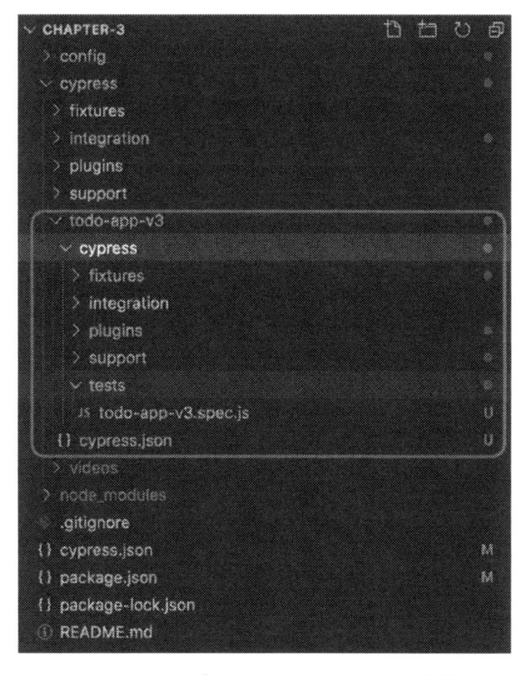

Figure 3.2 – todo-app-v3 project test folder

As shown in the preceding screenshot, we have modified the `integrationFolder` property in the `todo-app-v3` project to set the test folder from `cypress/integration` in the main tests folder to `cypress/tests` in the todo-app-v3 project.

cypress open --port <port-number>

By default, Cypress runs on port `8080`. Running the `cypress run` command while passing the `--port` option enables you to override the default port where the tests are run, to a specific port that is chosen by you.

The following code snippet is part of the `package.json` file located in the `chapter-03/` directory of this book's GitHub repository. Running the following command changes the default port that Cypress runs on:

```
"scripts": {
"cypress:open:changed-port": "cypress open --env
TransferProtocol='http' --port 3004"
  },
```

To run the previous Cypress script, you need to run the `npm run cypress:open:changed-port` command. Running this command will ensure that the tests are being run on port `3004`, instead of the port where Cypress runs its tests by default on the test runner:

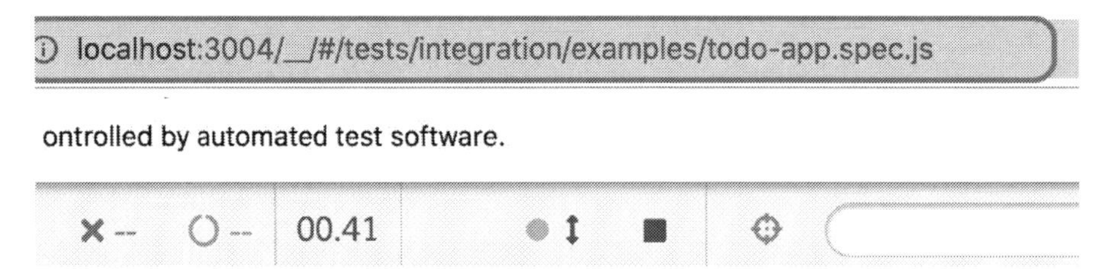

Figure 3.3 – Overriding the default Cypress tests port

The preceding screenshot shows how to run tests on port `3004` after an override using the `--port` option, which was passed to the `cypress run` command. The port being used here is for demonstration purposes only; any usable port on a user's machine can be passed as an override port for a Cypress application.

Using the cypress info command

Running the `cypress info` command on a Terminal will print the Cypress installation information and the environment configuration on the Terminal. The information that the command prints includes the following:

- Browsers that have been installed on the machine and that have been detected by Cypress.
- Information about the host operating system.
- The location of the Cypress binary cache.
- The location of the runtime data storage.
- Environment variables that have been prefixed with **CYPRESS** and that control configurations such as the system proxy.

Using the cypress version command

The `cypress version` command prints out the binary version of Cypress and the npm version of the Cypress module that's been installed. While most of the time, the versions should be the same, they can differ when the installed module, such as the binary version, was unable to be installed as a package module from npm, hence resulting in a difference in versions. The output from the `cypress version` command is shown in the following screenshot:

```
chapter-3 • ?  cypress version
Cypress package version: 4.7.0
Cypress binary version: 4.7.0
```

Figure 3.4 – cypress version command's output

The preceding screenshot shows both the Cypress package and binary version that have been installed on my machine. Both the package and binary versions of Cypress are the same versions.

Optional exercise for Cypress command usage

Using the **todoMVC** project defined in our project specifications, create a script that can run the following test scenarios:

- Headless tests using the edge browser.
- Tests on the test runner where the `TransferProtocol` environment variable is specified in `cypress.json` in the `chapter 03` root folder.

By the end of this exercise, you will understand how to run headed and headless tests, as well as how to add environment variables to scripts that we can use to execute different Cypress commands. You will also learn how to use different browsers to execute Cypress tests.

Recap – understanding basic Cypress commands

In this section, we learned how to use different Cypress commands to run Cypress using the command line or using the Cypress test runner, which runs using different browsers that have been installed on the system. We learned that although Cypress comes with default commands to run tests, we can extend these commands and increase the efficiency of running our tests by utilizing the commands and options available to customize Cypress for our use cases. We also provided an exercise so that you can apply the knowledge you've gained of using the `cypress run` and `cypress open` commands. In the next section, you will learn how to use the built-in Cypress debugger to view important debugging information that's necessary for troubleshooting errors using our terminals.

Cypress debugging on the command line

In this section, we will explore how to use the command line debugging properties of Cypress to troubleshoot the problems that we may encounter when running our tests. We will also explore the different debugging options that Cypress offers through the command line.

Cypress has a built-in debug module that can be exposed to users by passing debug commands before you run the tests using either `cypress run` or `cypress open`. To receive debugging output from the Terminal, the `DEBUG` environment variable needs to be set prior to the Cypress test runs in Mac or Linux environments.

The following scripts can be found in the `chapter-03/` root directory's `package.json` file and are used to show debug output when the commands are executed. The first script can be used to show debug output when the `cypress open` command is used to run tests, while the second script can be used to show debug output when the `cypress run` command is used to run tests:

```
"scripts": {
"cypress:open:debugger": "DEBUG=cypress:* cypress open --env
TransferProtocol='http'",
    "cypress:run:debugger": "DEBUG=cypress:* cypress run --
```

```
    env TransferProtocol='http'"
  },
}
```

As shown in the preceding commands, running `npm run cypress:open:debugger` will run the Cypress tests in a Terminal and log the debug output from the run. The second command, which can be run with `npm run cypress:run:debugger`, will run the debugger while running the tests on the Cypress test runner.

Cypress makes it easy to filter through the debug output since you can choose to have debugging information about specific modules, such as the Cypress server, the CLI, or the launcher modules.

The following script is located in the `package.json` file in the `chapter-03/` directory of this book's GitHub repository. When run, it will provide debug output for all the logs that are under the Cypress server module:

```
...
"scripts": {
"cypress:open:server-debugger": "DEBUG=cypress:server:* cypress
open --env TransferProtocol='http'"
}
...
```

Running the preceding command with `npm run cypress:run:server-debugger` will only output the debugger information related to the Cypress server. Using the filtering commands not only makes it easy to narrow down issues in Cypress, but also helps filter out noise, leaving logs that are important for debugging Cypress information and that will lead us to the source of the problem.

Optional exercise for Cypress debugging

Using the **todoMVC** project defined in our project's specifications, create a script that will run the following test scenarios:

- Debugging the Cypress CLI module
- Debugging the `cypress:server` project module

By the end of this exercise, you will have a grasp of the concepts of debugging in Cypress, and also have knowledge of how to create and run Cypress scripts in the `package.json` file.

Recap – Cypress debugging on the command line

In this section, we learned how to utilize Cypress to view additional information about our test runs by setting the `DEBUG` environment variable. We also learned how to utilize Cypress' `debug` variable to filter out the debug output that we require, and performed an exercise to extend our knowledge on debugging using the command line.

Summary

In this chapter, we learned about the `cypress open` and `cypress run` commands, as well as how the two commands can be chained with configuration options to extend their usage. We also learned how to check the Cypress information and Cypress versions that have been installed on our system. In the final section, we learned how to use Cypress to provide debug output and find out the cause of failures in our tests. In the next chapter, we will dive into writing Cypress tests and understanding the different parts of a test.

4
Writing Your First Test

Before you start this chapter, you need to have an understanding of how Cypress tests are run, different Cypress commands, how to set up Cypress, running Cypress on the command line, and how to use the test runner to open Cypress tests. This information was covered in the first three chapters, and will help you better understand the fundamentals that we will be building on in this chapter when writing our first test.

In this chapter, we will cover the basics of creating test files and writing a basic test, before we move on and write more complicated tests and assert various elements using Cypress.

We will cover the following topics in this chapter:

- Creating test files
- Writing your first test
- Writing practical tests
- Cypress' auto-reload feature
- Cypress assertions

By completing this chapter, you will be ready to learn how to debug running tests using the test runner.

Technical requirements

The GitHub repository for this chapter can be found at the following link:

`https://github.com/PacktPublishing/End-to-End-Web-Testing-with-Cypress`

The source code for this chapter can be found in the `chapter-04` directory.

Creating test files

All tests within Cypress must be within a test file for them to run. For a test to be considered useful, it must validate all the conditions that we have defined in the test and return a response stating whether the conditions have been met. Cypress tests are no exception to the process of writing tests, and all the tests that are written in a test file must have a set of conditions to be validated.

In this section, we will go through the process of writing a test file, starting from where a test file should be located in Cypress, different extensions that Cypress supports, and the file structures that test files written in Cypress should follow.

Testfiles location

Cypress creates test files by default when it is initialized in the `cypress/integration/examples` directory. However, these can be deleted as they are intended to show the proper format of utilizing different Cypress test types and assertions. Cypress allows you to be flexible when it comes to locating different modules and folder structures.

It is recommended that when you're working on your first project, you use the location mentioned in the previous paragraph to write your Cypress tests. To reconfigure the Cypress folder structures, you can change the Cypress default configuration and pass the new configuration into the `cypress.json` file. A good example of changing the default Cypress configuration would be to change our test directory from being located in `cypress/integration/examples to cypress/tests/todo-app` to elsewhere. To change the default directory, all we would need to do is change our `cypress.json` configuration, as shown here:

```
{
"integrationFolder": "cypress/tests"
}
```

The preceding code block shows the `integrationFolder` setting, which changes how the Cypress `tests` dictionary is configured.

Testfiles extensions

Cypress accepts different file extensions, which allows us to write tests that go beyond the normal JavaScript default format. The following file extensions are acceptable in Cypress tests:

- `.js`
- `.jsx`
- `.coffee`
- `.cjsx`

In addition to these, Cypress also supports ES2015 out of the box and CommonJS modules, which makes it possible for us to use keywords such as **import** and **require** without any additional configuration.

Testfile structure

Testfile structures in Cypress are similar to most of the other structures used to write tests or even normal JavaScript code. The structure of Cypress tests takes module imports and declarations into consideration, as well as the test body, which contains the tests. This can be seen in the following sample test file:

```
  // Module declarations
import {module} from 'module-package';

  // test body
describe('Test Body', () => {
    it('runs sample test', () => {
        expect(2).to.eq(2);
    })
})
```

As you can see, every test file needs to have the declarations at the top-most part of the test file. By doing this, the tests can be nested in the `describe` blocks, which specify the scope and the type of tests that will be run.

Creating our test file

Using the GitHub link located in the *Technical requirements* section, open the `chapter-04` folder. Follow these steps to create your first test file:

1. Navigate to the `integration` folder directory located inside the Cypress directory.
2. Create an empty test file called `sample.spec.js`.
3. For the purposes of this demonstration, we have created a `package.json` file in the `chapter-04` root directory for you. All you need to do is run the commands without worrying about how they work for now.
4. Launch the Cypress test runner with the `npm run cypress:run` command.
5. Check the test runner preview and confirm that the test file we added is visible.

Now, it's time for a quick recap.

Recap – creating test files

In this section, we learned how to create test files, how Cypress accepts different test file formats, and how to change the default directory of Cypress tests. We also learned the structure of a test and how Cypress borrows the format of tests from languages such as JavaScript. In the next section, you will focus on writing your first test.

Writing your first test

Cypress tests are no different than any other tests. As in all other tests, Cypress tests should pass when the expected result is consistent with what the application under test expects; it should fail when the expected result is not consistent with what the application should do. In this section, we will explore different types of tests, the structure of a test, and how Cypress understands the changes in a test file and reruns the tests. This section will also cover how to write practical tests.

Example test

In this section, we will look at the basic structure of a Cypress test. This remains standard in most of the tests that we will write during the course of this chapter. The following test checks that what we expect and what is returned are equal to `true`. It should pass when we run it:

```
describe('Our Sample Test', () => {
  it('returns true', () => {
    expect(true).to.equal(true);
  });
});
```

Here, we can see that the test has `describe()` and `it()` hooks. The hooks included in the Cypress tests come bundled by default from the **Chai** assertion library, which Cypress uses as its default assertion library. The hooks are used to help you to understand the different stages of the tests. The `describe` hook helps encapsulate different tests into one block, while the `it` hook helps us identify specific tests within a test block.

> **Important Note**
> The Chai assertion library is included in the Cypress framework as a package. It is the default assertion library that Cypress uses to verify the success or failure of tests.

Considering the test we saw in this section, we will now explore the different types of test classification in Cypress.

Test classification

Tests can be classified into the results they yield after they've been run. Cypress tests can also be classified according to their states. The tests can be in any of the following states:

- Passing
- Failed
- Skipped

We'll take a detailed look at these three categories in the next few sections.

Passing tests

A passing test is a test that correctly validates the input by matching it with the expected output. In Cypress, passing tests are clearly marked as passed, and this is visible on the command log and the Cypress test runner. Using the `sample.spec.js` file that we created earlier, we can create our first passing test, as shown in the following code block:

```
describe('Our Passing Test', () => {
  it('returns true', () => {
    expect(true).to.equal(true);
  });
});
```

To run the test while using the `chapter-04` directory as a reference, we can run the following command on the command-line interface:

```
npm run cypress:open
```

In this test, we are verifying that the input given, `true`, is similar to the test output that we expect, which is also `true`. This test might not be very useful, but its purpose is to show a passing test. The following screenshot shows a passing test:

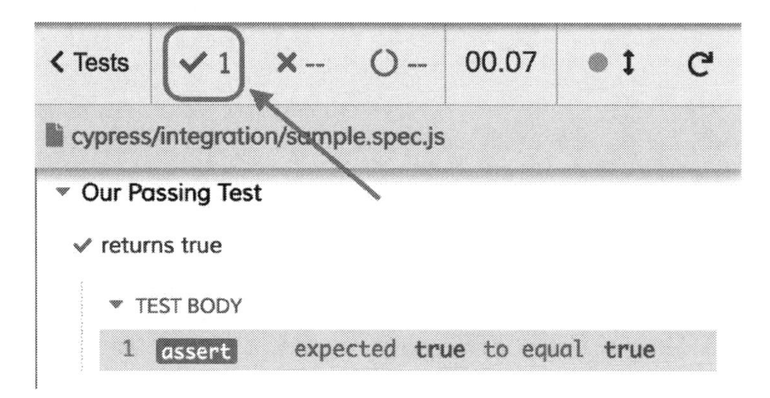

Figure 4.1 – Passing test

The preceding screenshot shows the result of passing the test in the command log. We can further verify that the test passes all the other conditions by looking at the green checkmark in the top-left corner.

Failing tests

Just like a passing test, a failing test also validates the test input against the test expectations and compares it to the result. A test failure occurs in the event that the expected result and the test input do not evaluate to the same thing. Cypress does a good job of displaying failing tests and describing what failed in the test. Using the same `sample.spec.js` file we created earlier, create a failing test, as shown in the following code block:

```
describe('Our Failing Test', () => {
  it('returns false, () => {
    expect(true).to.equal(false);
  });
});
```

To run the test , we will use the `chapter-04` directory as a reference, and then run the following command in the terminal:

```
npm run cypress:open
```

In this failing test, we are comparing a test input of `true` to a test expectation of `false`, which leads to a failing test set to `true`, which is not equal to `false`. The test automatically fails as it does not pass the validation that determines that our test passed. The following screenshot shows the result of our failing test in the command log:

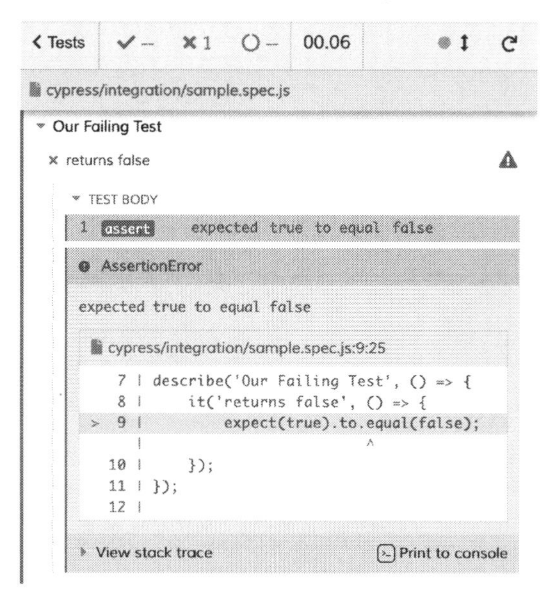

Figure 4.2 – Failing test

Looking at the command log, we can see that we have two tests: one that passes and one that fails. On the failing test, the Cypress command log shows the assertions that failed to meet our expectations. The test runner, on the other hand, goes ahead and shows us one failing test as a summary of our test run. When the test fails, Cypress allows us to read the exact exception that occurred. In this case, we can clearly see that the test failed at the assertion level due to an incorrect assertion.

Skipped tests

Skipped tests in Cypress are not executed. Skipped tests are used to omit tests that are either failing or that do not need to run when other tests are being executed. Skipped tests are suffixed with the `.skip` keyword after their test hook. We can skip tests that are in a whole block by skipping the test block with `describe.skip`, or just skip a single test by using `it.skip`. The following code block shows two tests in which the main `describe` block is skipped and another test that is skipped inside the `describe` block. The following code illustrates different ways of skipping Cypress tests:

```
describe.skip('Our Skipped Tests', () => {
    it('does not execute', () => {
        expect(true).to.equal(true);
    });
    it.skip('is skipped', () => {
        expect(true).to.equal(false);
    });
});
```

Here, we can see that we can skip either the whole code block or specific tests when we add `.skip` to either the `it` or `describe` hook. The following screenshot shows a skipped test:

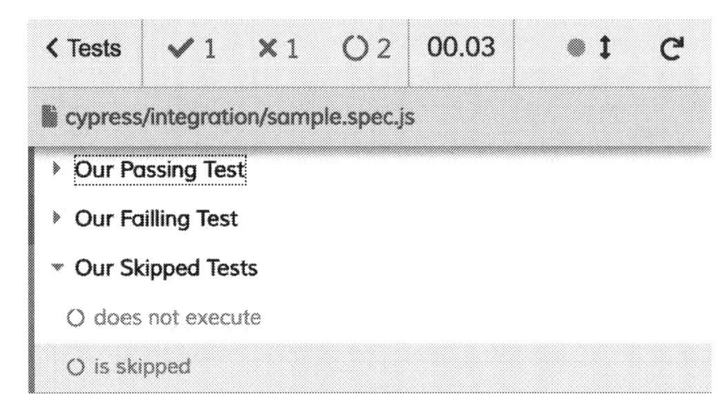

Figure 4.3 – Skipped test

Skipped tests are just shown as skipped in the command log and in the test runner; no activity takes place for a test block or a single test that has been skipped. The preceding screenshot shows the state of the skipped tests defined in our `sample.spec.js` file, which can be found in our `chapter-04` GitHub repository directory. Now that we know how to write different types of tests, we can dive into writing practical tests. But first, let's test our knowledge.

Exercise on tests classification

Using the knowledge you've gained by reading this section of this chapter, write tests that meet the following criteria:

- A passing test that asserts that a variable is of the `string` type
- A failing test that asserts a valid variable is equal to `undefined`
- A skipped test that checks whether a Boolean variable is `true`

Now, let's recap what we've covered in this section.

Recap – writing your first test

In this section, we learned how to identify different types of tests and looked at how the Cypress framework treats them. We learned what passing tests, failing tests, and skipped tests are. We also learned how the Cypress test runner displays the states of tests that have either passed, failed, or been skipped. Finally, we went through an exercise to test our knowledge of classifying tests. Now, let's move on to writing a practical test.

Writing practical tests

In the previous section, we went through the basics of understanding different classifications for tests in Cypress and what the results of the classifications are. In this section, we will focus on writing tests that go beyond asserting that a Boolean value is equal to another Boolean value.

For any test to have value, it needs to have three fundamental phases:

1. Setting up the desired state of the application
2. Executing the action to be tested
3. Asserting the state of the application after executed actions

In our practical tests, we will use our **Todo** application to write tests that correspond to the three fundamental phases required to write a meaningful test. To do this, we will complete the following steps:

1. Visit the Todo application page.
2. Search for an element.
3. Interact with the element.
4. Make an assertion on the application state.

These steps will guide the practical tests that we are about to write and will help us in having a the holistic view of Cypress tests.

Visiting the Todo application page

This step involves visiting the Todo application page, which is where we will run our test. Cypress provides a built-in `cy.visit()` command for navigating to web pages. The following code block shows the steps we need to follow to visit our Todo page. This code block can be found in the `chapter-04` folder of this book's GitHub repository, in the `practical-tests.spec.js` file:

```
describe('Todo Application tests', () => {
  it('Visits the Todo application', () => {
    cy.visit('http://todomvc.com/examples/react/#/')
  })
})
```

When this test runs, upon observing the command log, we will see the `visit` command, as well as the application that we just visited in the Cypress application preview on the right, as shown in the following screenshot:

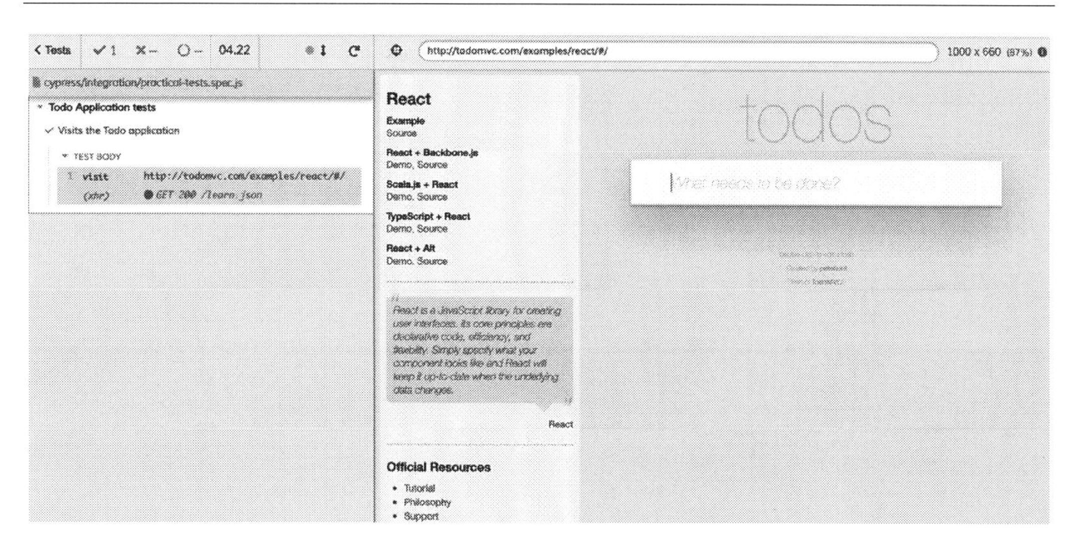

Figure 4.4 – Visiting the Todo application

Even though our application does not have any assertions, our test still passes as no error leading to the failure of our test has caused Cypress to throw an exception. Cypress commands are built to fail by default if they encounter an error, and this adds to the confidence we have when writing our tests.

Searching for an element

To make sure that Cypress performs some action in our application, we need to perform an action that will cause the application state to change. Here, we will search for a Todo application input element that is used to *add a Todo* item to our application. The following code block will search for the element that's responsible for adding a new Todo item and verify that it is present in the URL we just navigated to:

```
it('Contains todo input element', () => {
  cy.visit('http://todomvc.com/examples/react/#/')

  cy.get('.new-todo')
});
```

When the Cypress `cy.get()` command does not find the input element, an error will be thrown; otherwise, Cypress will pass the test. To get the input element, we do not need to verify that the element exists as Cypress already handles this using the **default assertions** that are chained in most Cypress commands.

> **Important Note**
>
> Default assertions in Cypress are built-in mechanisms that will cause a command to fail without the need for explicit assertions to be declared by the user. With these commands, Cypress takes care of the behavior of an exception if it's encountered while executing the said command.

The following screenshot shows Cypress searching for the Todo input element that is responsible for adding Todo items to our Todo list:

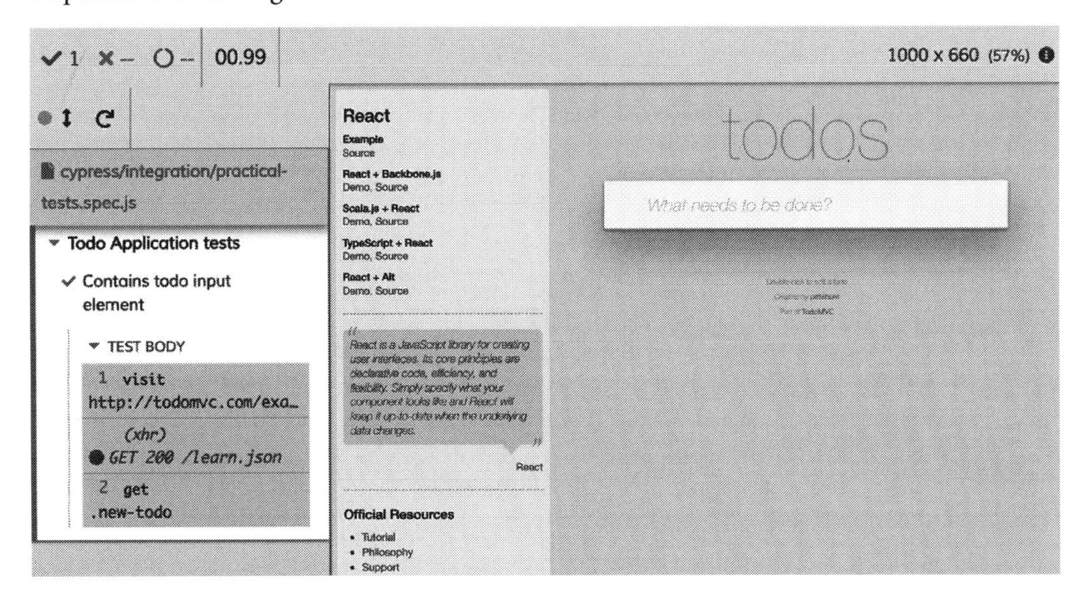

Figure 4.5 – Searching for the Todo input element

Here, we can verify that Cypress visited the Todo application URL, then checked that the input element that adds Todo items exists.

Interacting with the Todo input element

Now that we have confirmed we have an input element in our Todo application, it is time to interact with the application and change its state. To change the state of the Todo application, we will add a Todo item using the input element that we verified exists. Cypress chains commands together. To interact with our element, we will use the Cypress `.type()` command to send a string to the element and add the Todo item to the application state. The following code block will add a new Todo using the Todo input element:

```
it('Adds a New Todo', () => {
  cy.visit('http://todomvc.com/examples/react/#/')

  cy.get('.new-todo').type('New Todo {enter}')
});
```

The preceding code block builds on the previous code and uses the Cypress `type()` function to add a new Todo. Here, we also invoked the `{enter}` argument of the Cypress `type` method to simulate the *Enter* key functionality since the Todo application does not have a submit button to click for us to add a new Todo item. The following screenshot shows the added Todo item. With this item, we can verify that our test was successfully able to add a new Todo item. This item is visible on the Todo list:

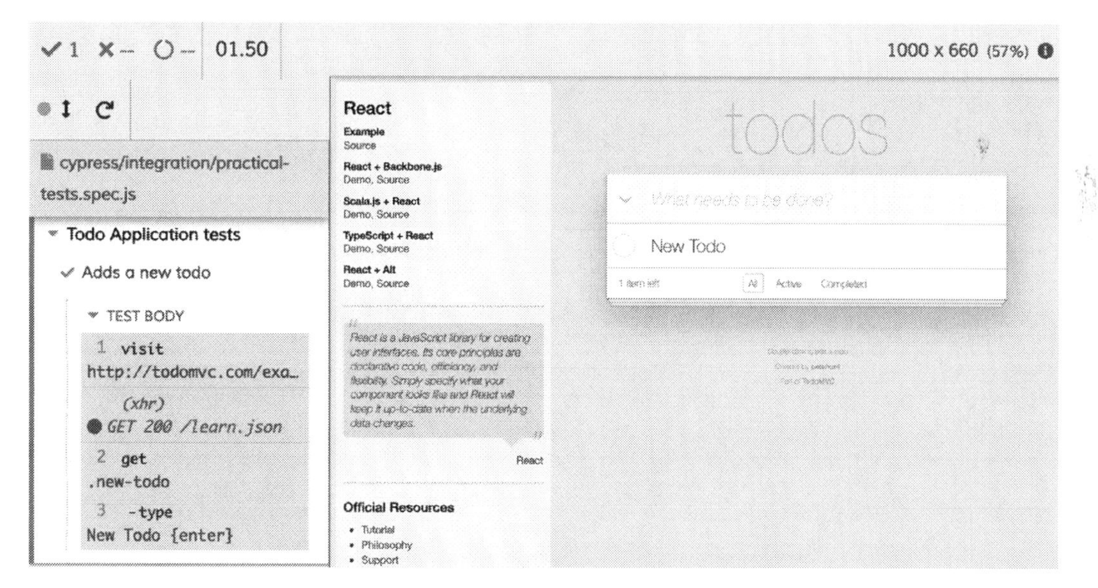

Figure 4.6 – Interacting with the Todo input element

Our test runner shows that a new Todo has been created. Again our test passes, even without an assertion, since the commands that have been run have passed the default Cypress assertions. Now, we need to assert that the application state has changed.

Asserting the application state

Now that we've added our Todo, we need to assert that our new Todo item has been added and that the application state has changed due to the addition of the Todo item. To do this, we need to add an assertion once we've added our Todo item. In the following code block, we will assert our changes to the application state. Here, we have added an assertion to check that the `.Todo-list` class, which holds the list items, is equal to `2`:

```
it('asserts change in application state', () => {
        cy.visit('http://todomvc.com/examples/react/#/')

        cy.get('.new-todo').type('New Todo {enter}')
        cy.get('.new-todo').type(Another Todo {enter}')
        cy.get(".todo-list").find('li').should('have.length', 2)
    });
```

To further validate our state changes, we can add more Todo items to verify that the number of items increases as we add Todo items.

In Cypress, we can use assertion functions such as `.should()` and `expect()`, which are bundled within the tools that make up Cypress. By default, Cypress extends all the functions that are in the Chai library, which is the default Cypress assertion library. The following screenshot shows two added Todo items and a confirmation note on the Cypress preview stating that the two added Todo items exist in the Todo list:

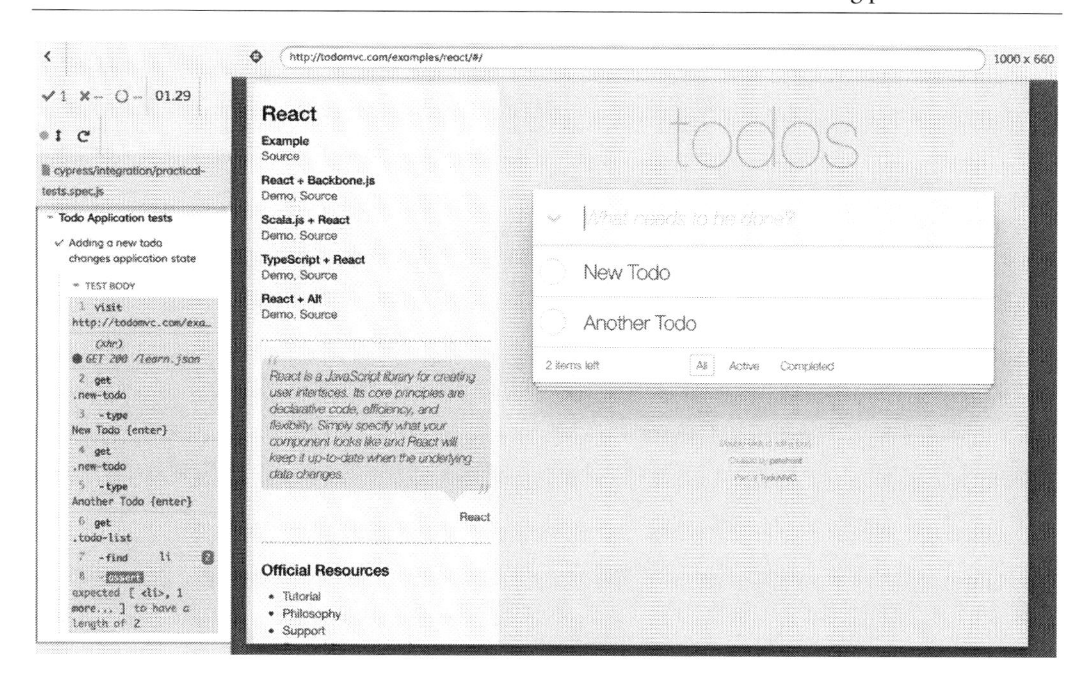

Figure 4.7 – Asserting the application state

In this test, we can verify that all the added Todos are visible on the Cypress app's preview page and that our assertion passes. We can now add more assertions, specifically to check that the name of the first Todo is `New Todo` and that the other added Todo is called `Another Todo`. To do this, we will add more assertions to our test and check specific details of our Todo items. In the following code block, we will verify that Cypress can check the names of the added Todo items; that is, *New Todo* and *Another Todo*:

```
it('asserts inserted todo items are present', () => {
    cy.visit('http://todomvc.com/examples/react/#/')

    cy.get('.new-todo').type('New Todo {enter}')
    cy.get('.new-todo').type('Another Todo {enter}')
    cy.get(".todo-list").find('li').should('have.length', 2)
    cy.get('li:nth-child(1)>div>label').should(
        'have.text', 'New Todo')
    cy.get('li:nth-child(2)>div>label').should(
        'have.text', 'Another Todo')
  });
```

In these assertions, we have used the Cypress `cy.get()` method to find the elements using their CSS classes and then identified the first and last added Todo items by their text.

Exercise on practical testing

Using the GitHub repository link mentioned in the *Technical requirements* section, write a test that navigates to the Todo application and add three new Todo items to it. Write tests that check that the Todo items that have been added exist by verifying their values and their quantity.

Recap – writing practical tests

In this section, we wrote our first practical test. Here, we visited a page, checked that the page had an input element, interacted with the element, and asserted that the application state changes. Having understood the flow of tests in Cypress, we can now move on and look at the features that make test writing interesting in Cypress, such as auto-reload.

Cypress' auto-reload feature

By default, Cypress watches for file changes and reloads the tests immediately when a file change is detected. This only happens if Cypress is running. The Cypress auto-reload feature comes in handy because you do not need to rerun the tests once you've made changes to their test files.

With the auto-reload feature, it is possible to have instant feedback and understand whether their changes were successful or whether their tests are failing. Due to this, this feature allows you to save time that would have otherwise been used for debugging tests or checking whether the changes that were made fixed the problem.

While Cypress' auto-reload feature is enabled by default, you may opt to turn it off and manually rerun the tests after making a change. Cypress allows you to stop watching for file changes. This can either be done by configuring the `cypress.json` file or by using Cypress' command-line configuration options. When using the `cypress.json` configuration file, the setting you must use to disable watching for file changes is as follows:

```
{
  "watchForFileChanges": "false"
}
```

This setting will persist and permanently disable file changes as long as Cypress is running, unless the configuration is altered or changed to `true`. The other option when it comes to disabling Cypress watching for the file changes is to use the command-line configuration option shown here:

```
cypress open --config watchForFileChanges=false
```

With this command, Cypress will temporarily stop watching for file changes, and will only change this behavior when we stop the execution of Cypress on our terminal window. Cypress will then continue to watch for file changes and auto-reload whenever changes are made to a test file.

Recap – Cypress' auto-reload feature

In this section, we learned how Cypress utilizes the auto-reload feature to watch for file changes and immediately reload and rerun when any changes take place in our test files. We also learned how to easily turn off the auto-reload feature in Cypress either by permanently disabling it using the `cypress.json` file or by passing the command in the command-line configuration when running our tests. Next, we will be looking at Cypress assertions.

Cypress assertions

As we learned in the previous section, when writing our first test, assertions exist to describe the desired state of the application. Assertions in Cypress behave like guards to the tests in that they validate that the desired state and the present state are the same. Cypress assertions are unique as they are retried when Cypress commands are running until a timeout is reached or until an element is found.

Cypress assertions originate from the **chai**, **chai-jquery** and **sinon-chai** modules, which come bundled with the Cypress installation. Cypress also allows you to write custom assertions using the Chai plugins. However, in this section, we will focus on the default assertions that come bundled with Cypress, and not on the custom assertions that can be extended as plugins.

We can write Cypress assertions in two ways: either by explicitly defining subjects or by implicitly defining subjects. Cypress recommends implicitly defining subjects in assertions as they are immediate to the element that the Cypress commands are working on. The following are how assertions are classified in the Cypress framework:

- Implicit subjects: `.should()` or `.and()`
- Explicit subjects: `expect()`

Let's look at each of them in detail.

Implicit subjects

The `should` or `and` commands are Cypress commands, which means they can directly act on the immediately yielded subjects from Cypress. The commands can also be chained with other Cypress commands, which makes them easy to work with while at the same time guaranteeing an immediate response when invoking them. The following code block demonstrates how to test implicit subjects. Here, we will use the output of the `cy.get` command to make assertions in our test:

```
describe('Cypress Assertions', () => {
    it('Using Implicit subjects - should', () => {
        cy.visit('http://todomvc.com/examples/react/#/')

        // Check if todo input element has expected
        // placeholder value
        cy.get(".new-todo").should('have.attr', 'placeholder',
        'What needs to be done?')
    });
});
```

Here, we are using the `should()` command to assert that the input element for the Todo items has a placeholder value. The `should` command is chained from the `cy.get()` command. This not only makes it easy to work with, but also reduces the amount of code that is required to assert that the placeholder is what it is. In the following code block, we are combining different assertions of an implicit subject that will be returned by the `cy.get` command:

```
it('Using Implicit subjects - and()', () => {
        cy.visit('http://todomvc.com/examples/react/#/')

```

```
        // Check if todo input element has expected
        // placeholder value
        cy.get(".new-todo")
         .should('have.attr', 'placeholder',
          'What needs to be done?')
        .and('have.class', 'new-todo')
    });
```

Here, we have used the `.and()` Cypress command to further verify that the element that was just yielded has both a placeholder and a CSS class called `new-todo`. With these implicit assertions, we can verify that by using implicit subjects, we can chain off multiple commands from the same yielded response from Cypress, and also assert different items. The following code block shows code assertions that have been made by using explicit subjects where we have to declare each subject that we are asserting:

```
it('Using Explicit subjects', () => {
        cy.visit('http://todomvc.com/examples/react/#/')

        cy.get(".new-todo").should( ($elem) => {
        expect($elem).to.have.class('new-todo')
        expect($elem).to.have.attr('placeholder','What needs
        to be done?')
        })
    });
```

As you can see, when using implicit subjects, we can make cleaner assertions and reduce the amount of code we write. In this code block, every assertion has to be on the same line and acted upon individually.

Explicit subjects

We use `expect()` when we want to assert specific subjects that we define when running a test. Explicit subjects are common in **unit tests** and are great when there is a need to perform some logic before we perform the assertion or even have several assertions for the same subject. The following code block shows explicit subject assertion using the `expect` method:

```
it('can assert explicit subjects', () => {
  const eqString = 'foo';
  expect(eqString).to.eq('foo');
```

```
    expect(eqString).to.have.lengthOF(3);
    expect(eqString).to.be.a('string');
  })
```

This code block shows an explicit comparison of the instantiated `string` to our expectations. The declared `string` is an explicit subject, which means it can be asserted more than once and also manipulated before it performs the assertions.

For complex assertions, we can use the `.should()` method to assert explicit subjects. This allows a callback function to be passed with the subject that has been yielded as the first argument. We can add assertions inside the `should` function like so:

```
  it('Using Should with Explicit subjects', () => {
          cy.visit('http://todomvc.com/examples/react/#/')
          cy.get(".new-todo").should( ($elem) => {
          expect($elem).to.have.class('new-todo')
          })
    });
```

Here, we have visited the URL, then used the yielded element from `cy.get('new-todo')` to assert that a CSS class with the name `new-todo` exists. This test allows us to query for an element and also write different assertions for the subject as the need arises.

Exercise–implicit and explicit subjects

Using the knowledge you've obtained from this section and by using the GitHub repository link mentioned in the *Technical requirements* section as a reference point, complete the following exercise.

Navigate to the Todo application URL (`http://todomvc.com/examples/react/#/`) and add a Todo:

- Write a test using implicit subject assertions to assert that the Todo has been added, and that the name you entered is the same name that is displayed on the Todo items list.
- On the Todo app URL, mark a Todo as completed. Then, using the explicit subject's assertion, write a test to verify that the completed Todo has been marked as completed.

Recap – Cypress assertions

In this section, we learned how to assert both explicit and implicit subjects and looked at how different and similar they are. We also learned that different assertion types can be used for different subjects. We then had the chance to carry out an exercise to practice our skills of asserting implicit and explicit subjects.

Summary

In this chapter, we learned how to classify tests in Cypress by understanding what passing, failing, and skipped tests mean and how Cypress views and represents tests in the test runner and command log. We also learned about the structure of the test file and the acceptable file extensions for Cypress tests. We then wrote our first practical tests, which tested that a Todo application can add, delete, and mark a Todo as completed. The highlight of this chapter was learning how Cypress watches for file changes and how we can carry out our assertions in Cypress either by explicitly asserting our test subjects or implicitly asserting them. By completing this chapter, you know how to write a basic test in Cypress by working with elements and understanding the assertions that are available. In the next chapter, we will learn how to debug running tests in Cypress and the tools that we can use for that purpose.

5
Debugging Cypress Tests

Debugging is the ability to identify and remove bugs from software applications. Having knowledge of debugging in Cypress and learning how to interpret Cypress' debugging output is critical to working with the Cypress framework. Cypress prides itself on its ability to give immediate feedback about whether tests have passed or failed. For Cypress to achieve an instant feedback mechanism, it has to be effective in the way the debug messages are structured in order to provide the user ease of interpretation.

To be able to excel in this chapter, you need to have read the previous chapters as they will help you gain knowledge of how tests run, how Cypress works, and the different ways in which we can run Cypress tests. In this chapter, we will focus on debugging Cypress tests while running them in headed mode through a test runner.

While this chapter will explore debugging Cypress using the test runner, Cypress comes bundled with other debugging tools that we might not necessarily cover in this chapter, since they have either been covered in the previous chapters or are outside the scope of this book. In this chapter, we will learn how Cypress debugging works in the test runner. To do this, we will cover the following topics:

- Understanding page events
- Understanding errors on a test runner
- Understanding time travel on executed tests
- Understanding test snapshots
- Understanding the console debug output
- Special debug commands

Once you've worked through each of these topics, you will be ready to start working on the second part of this book, which involves writing Cypress tests using a **test-driven development** (**TDD**) approach.

Technical requirements

The GitHub repository for this chapter can be found at `https://github.com/PacktPublishing/End-to-End-Web-Testing-with-Cypress`.

The source code for this chapter can be found in the `chapter-05` directory.

Understanding page events

Cypress logs every main event that takes place when the tests are running. It can detect when a URL is changing, when a button is clicked, or even when an assertion is being made. Page events capture the important events that the DOM goes through when a test is running.

To demonstrate how page events work, we will use our Todo application, as we did in the previous chapter. Following the `chapter-05` directory in our GitHub repository, we will create our test file in the Cypress integration subdirectory and name it `debugging.spec.js`. We will then create our test in the newly created spec file, which will navigate to the Todo application, add a todo item, and check for the page events that pop up in our Cypress test runner. The following code block will handle adding the todo item to our application:

```
it('can add a todo', () => {
      cy.get(".new-todo").type("New Todo {Enter}");
      cy.get(".todo-list").find('li').should('have.length',
      1)
  });
```

In this test, we are adding a todo item and checking that the item we've added can be viewed from our list of todo items. The following screenshot shows an XHR page event:

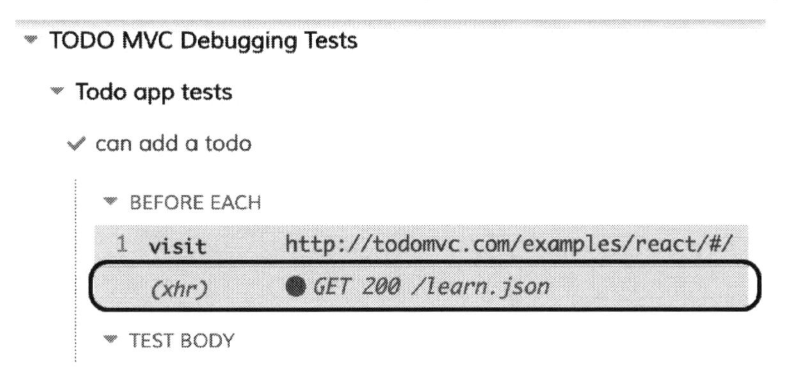

Figure 5.1 – XHR page event

The preceding screenshot shows part of the command log for the preceding test. The highlighted section, named `xhr`, is the page event for loading a new page in Cypress. The page event is automatically detected by the Cypress mechanism and is automatically logged – not as a command that needs to be executed, but as an event that has triggered a change in the application's state.

Cypress logs page events for the following:

- Submitting forms
- Loading new pages
- XHR requests for network calls
- Hash changes for test URLs

To identify Cypress page events, we need to look for logs in the Cypress command log that are gray and have no kind of numbering, such as the commands that are within a Cypress test being executed.

Recap – understanding page events

In this section, we covered what page events are, when and how they are logged, and how to identify them in Cypress. We also learned that page events are useful in tracing the main events that took place when a test was being executed. In the next section, we will look at how to obtain further debugging information when a test throws an error. We will do this by understanding the error messages that can be thrown.

Understanding errors on a test runner

In this section, we will dissect Cypress errors on the test runner, thus unpacking the contents of the errors thrown by Cypress and how to interpret them. We will cover different types of information that are present in Cypress errors, including the error name, the error message, the code frame file, the stack trace, the print to console option, and learn more. Understanding errors in Cypress will not only help us write better tests but also guide us through the debugging process when our tests fail.

Cypress excels when it comes to logging exceptions in a test failure event. Cypress not only logs information about which tests are failing but goes ahead and drills into specific information about the error that was encountered. Errors such as successful test executions are visible on the Cypress command log and provide descriptive pieces of information that could have led to the error being encountered. At times, Cypress even prints suggestions of what needs to be done to resolve the errors on the command log.

In this section, we will add a test to `debugging.spec.js` that will throw an error when it is run in Cypress. In the following test, we will explore the information that Cypress provides when an error is encountered, and also try to understand why that information is relevant to the process of debugging:

```
it('Error Test: can add a todo', () => {
      cy.get(".new-todo").type("New Todo {Enter}");
      cy.get(".todo-list").find('li').should('have.length',
      2)
  });
```

This test should intentionally throw an error as we are expecting the number of todo items to equal `2`, although we have only added a single todo item called `New Todo`.

Every error that is thrown by Cypress will contain the following pieces of information. These will help you identify where the problem is coming from and what caused the error that Cypress is throwing:

- **Error name**
- **Error message**
- **Code frame file**
- **Code frame**
- **Stack trace**
- **Print to console option**
- **Learn more (optional)**

Let's look at each of these in detail.

Error name

Cypress throws different kinds of errors, depending on the error that it has encountered. Errors in Cypress are identified by their types and they can be categorized by types such as Cypress errors and assertion errors, among others. The type of error that Cypress throws helps with debugging. This is because we can fully understand whether the test is failing from the tests that are running or from an error that Cypress has internally encountered. This error is shown in *Figure 5.2* referenced as *1* with the Error name.

Error message

With every error comes a message. This message gives a detailed explanation of what went wrong when the test was running. Error messages differ from test to test. While some messages may be straightforward and tell you what went wrong, others will go a step further and even detail the steps that you can take to fix the errors. Some error messages contain a **Learn more** section, which will direct you to the Cypress documentation that is related to the error that has been encountered. This error message is shown in *Figure 5.2* referenced by *2*.

Code frame file

This is the file that contains the error that Cypress has encountered. The file is shown as the topmost item of the stack trace. The code frame file is displayed with the line number and the column number that is highlighted in the Cypress error frame. When the code frame file on the stack trace is clicked, it will open in the preferred editor and highlight the line and the column where the error occurred, if the editor that was used to open the file supports code highlighting. We can see Code Frame File in *Figure 5.2*, which is referenced as number *3*.

Code frame

This is the code snippet that Cypress has flagged to be the cause of the error that occurred. It can be found in the code frame file mentioned previously. Cypress highlights the specific line that is problematic to executing the test in the code frame snippet, as well as the column. We can identify the code frame leading to the failure by checking the code snippet referenced as *4* in *Figure 5.2*.

Stack trace

The stack trace shows the different methods that were being executed when an error occurred, leading to an exception. In Cypress errors, you can toggle the stack trace, which can be found below the code frame in the error. This should show you the functions that were being executed by the test when it encountered an error and failed. Number *5* in *Figure 5.2* shows the stack trace region.

Print to console

Cypress errors also offer you the option to print the error that was encountered by the DevTools console. The option to print the encountered errors to Command Prompt allows us to select a line within the stack trace and print it to the console. We can see this in Figure 5.2 as 6.

Learn more

As we mentioned earlier, some of the test failures print a **Learn more** link, which, when clicked, gives us directions to the relevant Cypress documentation for the error that occurred. Cypress failures provide the **Learn more** link when the error might require more than just the assertion being adjusted or an expectation that is under test:

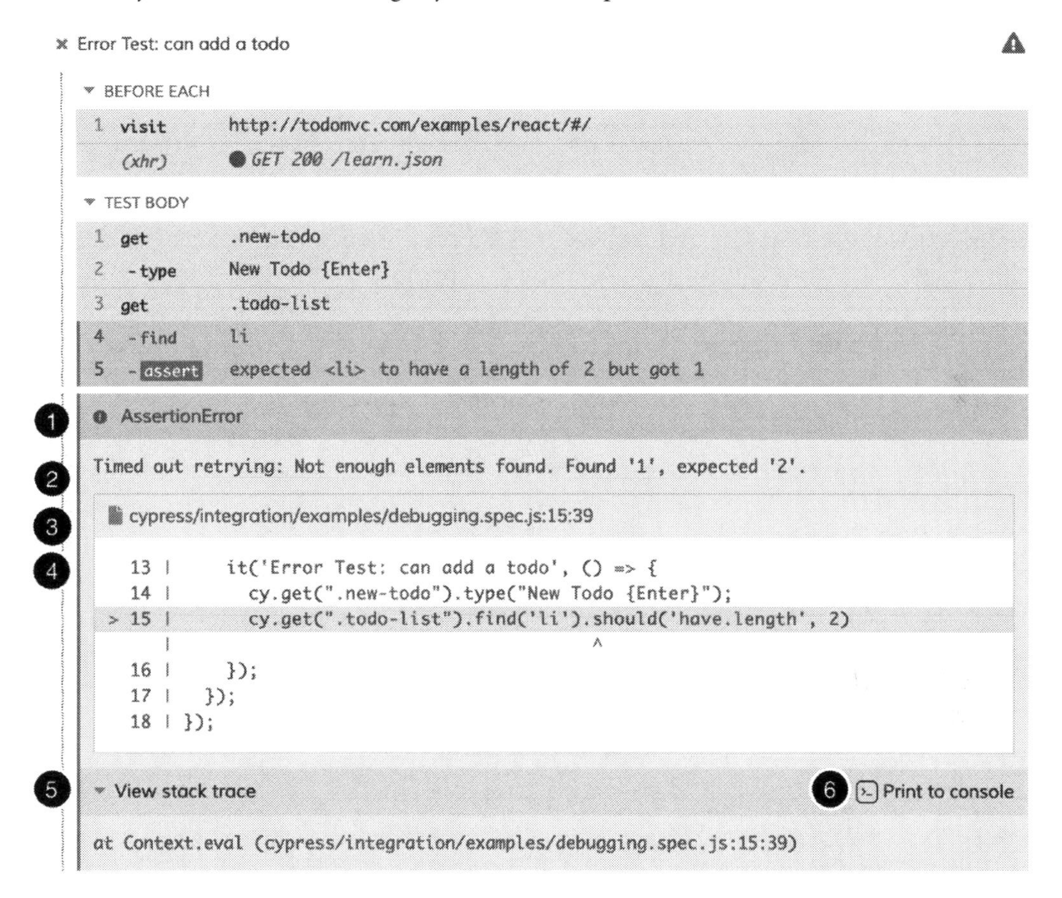

Figure 5.2 – Information that's present for test errors

The preceding screenshot shows the chronological structure of the error information that is displayed when a test throws an exception. As we can see, the test only adds one todo item to the todo list but expects to find two. The error occurs on the test assertion as Cypress expects two items but only one has been found, leading to the error.

The information provided by a failing test is crucial to the process of debugging. This is because not only does it become easy to identify why the tests are failing, but it also helps us understand where changes need to be made for us to restore the tests from a failing state to a passing state.

Recap – understanding errors on a test runner

In this section, we learned how informative Cypress errors are. We got to investigate different pieces of information that are embedded inside the Cypress error messages and their purpose in the debugging process. Knowing how Cypress presents its errors when they occur allows us to know how to deal with Cypress errors and understand where these errors are coming from. In the next section, we will look at the time travel feature of Cypress.

Understanding time travel on executed tests

Time travel, just like in sci-fi movies but now in the context of tests, is the ability to move back to a state that a test was in while being executed. As Cypress tests execute, they create DOM snapshots that we can use to travel back in time and check the state of our tests at different times and when different actions took place. With time travel, it is possible to check whether an expected action takes place and how it took place. Time travel also allows us to investigate and audit what actions were taken when the test was running and why errors occurred.

To investigate time travel in Cypress tests, we will navigate to our `chapter-05` folder in this book's GitHub repository and create a new test in the `debugging.spec.js` file, which we created previously. The following code block is a test that will mark added todo items as completed. With time travel, we can identify the different states of the application as we add todo items, and then mark them as completed:

```
it('can mark a todo as completed', () => {
        cy.get(".new-todo").type("New Todo {Enter}");
        cy.get(".new-todo").type("Another New Todo {Enter}");
        cy.get('.todo-list>li:nth-
        child(1)').find('.toggle').click();
        cy.get('.todo-list>li:nth-
        child(2)').find('.toggle').click();
    });
```

The preceding code block adds two todo items to the todo list and then marks the todo items as completed. Using the Cypress time travel feature, we can refer to Cypress to check the states of when we were adding the first todo item and even when we were adding the second todo item. By using the time travel feature, as shown in the following screenshot, we can further validate that both items were in the correct state before they were marked as completed, and that proper navigation was done in the process of doing so:

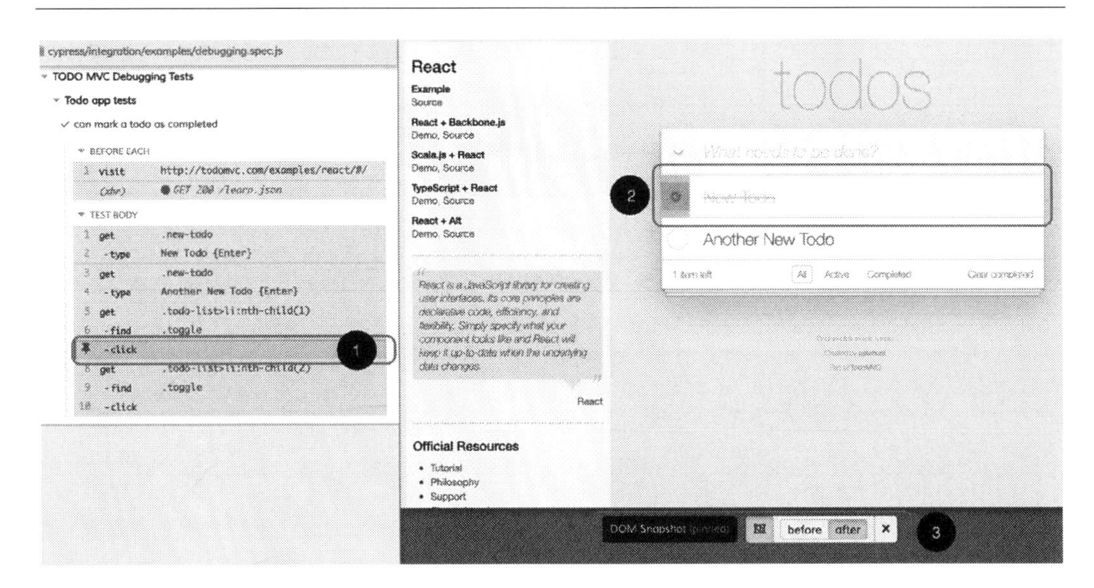

Figure 5.3 – Time travel and DOM snapshotting in a test

In the preceding screenshot, we can see that the test has already finished running and has already passed. We can also see that we can step back in time and investigate what was happening when the first todo item was clicked inside the todo list. Since Cypress can step back in time and show us the DOM at that particular point in time, we can actually verify the steps that were taken to reach the end result of the test – whether it was a test pass or a test failure. The numbers indicated show the main parts of the Cypress time travel mechanism and the order in which the events took place.

The first step in time travelling is waiting for the test run to be complete, then selecting the step that you want to time travel back to. Cypress not only shows the test steps but also allows you to pin the DOM snapshot of the step to the Cypress preview window.

After selecting the time travel step, the step of interest that we have selected is pinned as a DOM snapshot. We can view the step in the state it was in and in the new state that it was transformed into after the action took place. This can be seen in the preview window of the preceding screenshot.

The third step in the time travel inspection process is to choose between **after** and **before** for the DOM snapshot. Toggling between **after** and **before** shows changes within the DOM snapshots. This toggling helps us understand how the actions of the Cypress step that we are inspecting changed the DOM at that particular stage. When we are done with our inspection, we can move on to the next execution step and pin the state of the test at that particular step of execution.

> **Important Note**
>
> Cypress time travel does not work when the test is still executing and has not passed or failed. For proper results, you must wait for the execution to be completed before you see the end results of all the relevant steps.

Recap – understanding time travel on executed tests

In this section, we learned how Cypress provides us with a time travel feature so that we can go back to the different steps that Cypress took to execute our tests. Time traveling in Cypress allows us to check the steps that Cypress took to declare our tests either as failed or passed. We also got the chance to see how the time travel feature works with the snapshot feature, which we will cover in the next section.

Understanding test snapshots

We briefly covered the concept of snapshots when we explained the time travel process in Cypress. However, this does not mean we have exhausted the advantages of the Snapshots feature.

Snapshots are powerful as they give us a sneak peek into how the test executes and into the steps that it took, which either lead to a failure state or to a success state in the test. When we pin DOM snapshots, Cypress freezes the test and highlights all the actions that were taken. The pinned snapshots allow us to inspect the state of the DOM, while at the same time view all the events that took place in that particular step. In the preceding screenshot, for example, in *step 2*, there's an **event hitbox** that shows that the first todo item was clicked. The following screenshot shows how Cypress interprets events that take place as a test is running:

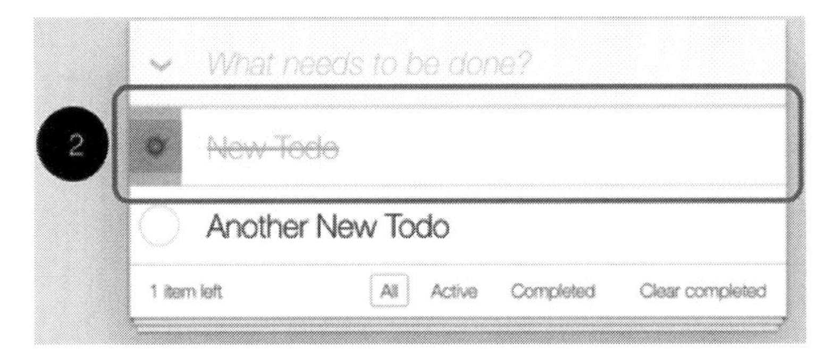

Figure 5.4 – An event hitbox for a toggled todo item

The preceding screenshot shows the event hitbox in action. Here, we can see a click event took place that affects the application state of the todo application.

> **Important Note**
>
> The event hitbox is a highlight that pops up on pinned Cypress snapshots to show that the test interacted with the element. The event hitbox can be triggered by Cypress events such as the `.click()` method.

The **Snapshots** menu allows us to toggle between the states of the snapshot. If an event took place that changed the DOM, we can toggle to see the state before the change took place and toggle to see the state after the change took place. The **before** snapshot toggle will display the state before any event that the selected test step triggered. On the other hand, the **after** toggle will show the state of the application after an event has been triggered from the selected step. The following screenshot shows a toggle for the pinned DOM snapshot, which shows what the snapshot looked like before an event and what it will look like after an event takes place:

Figure 5.5 – ADOM snapshot menu

In the preceding screenshot, we can see the **Snapshot** menu items. The first window-like icon will hide or show the **event hitbox** on the pinned DOM snapshot, while the **before** and **after** menus are used to show the transition of the DOM of the selected step. The **close** icon of the **Snapshot** menu, when clicked, unpins the DOM snapshot and reverts it back to the completed step of the tests without any pinned DOM snapshots.

> **Important Note**
>
> How the **before** and **after** events of the snapshot menu items are displayed depends on the event that took place. In events where the action has transformed the state of the DOM, then both the before and after snapshots will be different. When the action that was performed does not directly change the DOM: it is possible to have similar snapshots for both the before and after states of the test step.

Recap – understanding test snapshots

In this section, we learned how Cypress stores important debugging information in the DOM snapshots after every test run. We also learned how to utilize Cypress snapshots to check the before and after states of a test step, and then use this in the investigation process of debugging. In the next section, we will learn how to utilize the console's debug output for information.

Understanding the console debug output

In this section, we will understand how to leverage Cypress' console debug output to understand application state changes. We will open and interact with the console output in the browser's console. Understanding the output in the browser's console will allow us to debug tests even better, since we can investigate issues that are thrown as errors by Cypress and resolve them quickly.

Cypress is excellent at providing debugging information. Since all the information that's provided by the snapshots might not be enough, Cypress provides an additional step so that you can view the information of a specific step and its impact on elements. To view the console debug output, we will need to open our DevTools. To open the DevTools console of our Cypress test browsers, we need to follow certain steps, all of which will be discussed in the following sections.

macOS

To open the **DevTools** console of your Cypress test browser on macOS, follow these steps:

1. Hold the trackpad down with two fingers while on the Cypress test browser preview.
2. Select the **Inspect** option from the pop-up menu.
3. Select the **Console** tab from the **DevTools** console.

You can also use the *Option* + *J* shortcut to open the **DevTools** menu on Mac.

Windows/Linux OS

To open the **DevTools** console of your Cypress test browser on Windows and Linux OS, follow these steps:

1. Right-click on the Cypress test browser while on the Cypress test preview.
2. Select the **Inspect** option from the browser pop-up menu.
3. Select the **Console** tab from the **DevTools** console.

You can also open it using the *Shift* + *Ctrl* + *J* shortcut on either Windows operating systems or Linux to open the **DevTools** console.

Once you can see the console output, select a test step, as shown in the following screenshot:

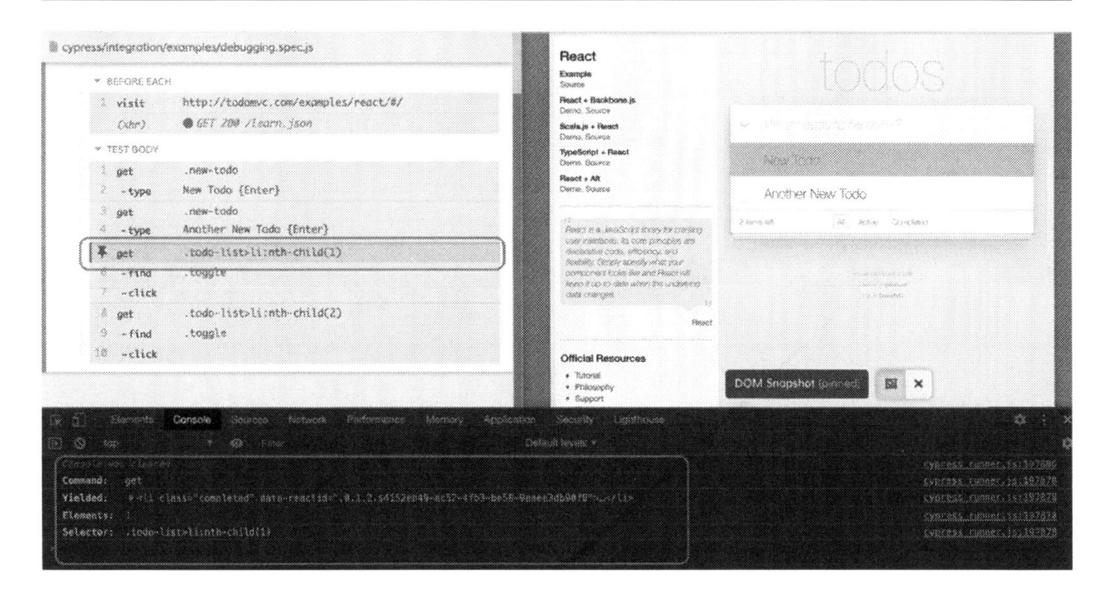

Figure 5.6 – The debug output on a browser console

The preceding screenshot shows the output of the selected Cypress command on Command Prompt. As we can see, when a specific command step is clicked, the DOM snapshot is pinned to the Cypress browser's preview screen. Pinning the DOM snapshot allows us to interact with the elements on the pinned snapshot uninterrupted.

In the preceding screenshot, we selected the `get` method and the first todo item, which can be identified by the `.todo-list>li:nth-child(1)` CSS selector. We can also see that the Cypress `get` method finds the CSS selector for the first todo item and toggles it to completed. Looking through the console debug information, we can see the additional information that Cypress printed on the console that is related to the action step and is now pinned to the DOM.

In the **Console** area, we can see the following:

- **Command**: This is the command that we issued. In our case, it was a `cy.get()` command.
- **Yielded**: This prints the statement that was returned by the command that was invoked. In our case, it will print out the same as what the input was. This is because we are not changing the state of the element with our command.
- **Elements**: This prints the elements that were returned from our `get` command. In our case, we only have one element that was found by using our CSS selector. However, if we had more than one element, we would be able to see the elements that were found.
- **Selector**: This refers to the CSS selector that we used to identify our todo item in the DOM.

> **Important Note**
>
> The information that's displayed on the console can change due to the different commands that are issued and inspected. This is not standard for all the Cypress commands that are inspected on the console log.

Using this debugging information and combining it with debug information from the methods we covered earlier will give you an idea of which Cypress tests are failing and why. In most cases, you only need to learn how to read the common Cypress errors to understand how the errors are thrown and why those errors appear.

Recap – understanding the console debug output

In this section, we learned how to utilize the console debug output in Cypress to understand application state changes. We also learned how to open and access the console information and interact with it. In the next section, we will learn how to utilize Cypress' special debugging commands.

Special debugging commands

If jumping through commands is not your thing, or you are finding it difficult to understand how travelling back in time shows you the order of execution in a test, Cypress has got your back. Cypress includes commands that are helpful for debugging and even gives you the options that you would have when using normal code debuggers. The two commands that we will be exploring in this section are as follows:

- `cy.debug()`
- `cy.pause()`

Using these Cypress debug commands, we can understand how to debug Cypress from the tests themselves. These two special debugging commands will allow us to directly control the debug process as we execute our tests. Having the ability to stop execution within the tests themselves gives us the advantage of only having to debug the specific sections that are throwing errors in Cypress.

cy.debug

The `cy.debug()` command is, by default, the debugging command that Cypress offers out of the box. The command will log onto the console and will log the output of the command that it has chained off. To use the `cy.debug()` command, you need to chain it from any `cy` command or use it as a standalone Cypress command. In our context, we will be using the command by chaining it from the `cy.get()` command.

This command pauses the execution of the test when it is called, and also displays the option of systematically stepping forward from a command and pausing the debugger from the current execution step. In reality, the debugger allows us to execute the test at our desired speed while inspecting what happens when a step is executed. In addition to the debugger interface, this Cypress command also displays verbose on the console output and displays information such as the command name, the type of command, and even the subject that we have chained our debugger from.

Now that we have added both of our todo items and inspected both the console log and the Cypress test runner preview pane, we can add the debugger. The following code block shows a test that marks a todo item as complete. However, instead of executing the whole test, we will open the debugger after adding the second todo item:

```
it('Special commands-debug : can mark a todo as completed',
() => {
        cy.get(".new-todo").type("New Todo {Enter}");
        cy.get(".new-todo").type("Another New Todo
        {Enter}").debug();
        cy.get('.todo-list>li:nth-
        child(1)').find('.toggle').click();
        cy.get('.todo-list>li:nth-
        child(2)').find('.toggle').click();
    });
```

In the preceding code block, we want to check the state of our application after the second todo item has been added. The following screenshot shows an open debugger after the second todo item was added:

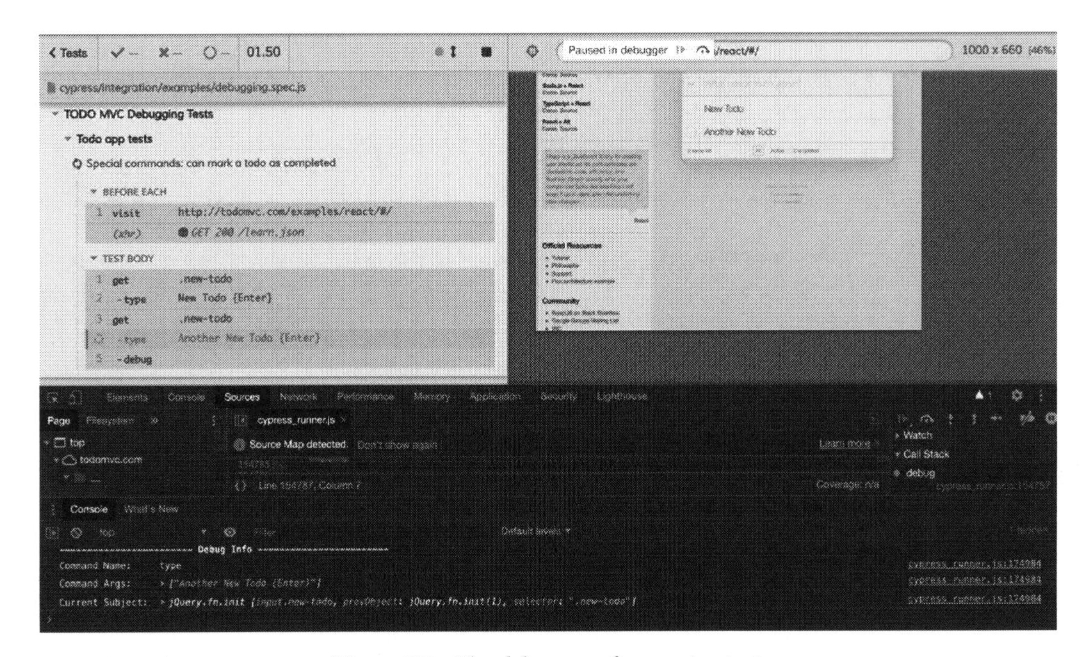

Figure 5.7 – The debugger of a running test

As we can see, the debugger pauses our running test after the second todo item is added. Here, we can observe that we can interact with the application and inspect elements at our own pace once the debugger has paused our running test. With the debugger in place, we can see the application state changes, along with additional debug information, displayed on the console output. Once we've finished inspecting the state, we can either remove the `.debug()` command or place it in another line that we wish to inspect.

cy.pause

The Cypress `pause` command works very similar to the `cy.debug()` command but instead of being chained to other commands, it can be used independently, just like a debugger. When the `pause` command is used, Cypress slows its execution and only executes the next step when the forward button is clicked. Just like the debugger, the Cypress `pause` command gives control to the person executing the tests and allows them to investigate every test step. The following code block shows a test that marks a todo item as completed. However, before execution is complete, we pause the test after adding the first todo item:

```
it('Special commands - Pause: can mark a todo as completed', ()
=> {
      cy.get(".new-todo").type("New Todo {Enter}");
      cy.pause();
      cy.get('.todo-list>li:nth-
      child(1)').find('.toggle').click();
  });
```

Here, we have added a single todo item and then paused the execution before marking it as completed:

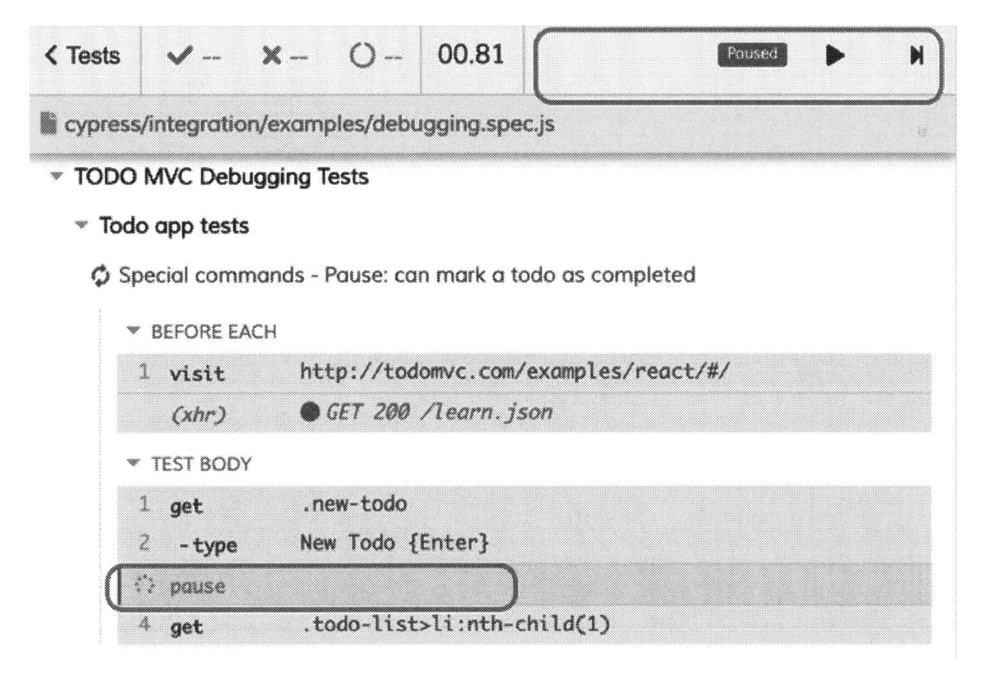

Figure 5.8 – The pause menu of a running test

As we can see, immediately after adding our todo item, execution is halted until we press the **step-forward** button in the **pause** menu. This appears on the top part of the test commands section. When all the steps have been executed, the test will exit and either pass or fail, depending on the output of the steps that were executed. In our case, we have a passing test – hurray!

> **Important Note**
>
> Cypress special debugging commands should only be used when we are investigating the state of the tests that are running or for debugging purposes. They should not be used in tests that are running in **continuous integration** (**CI**) as they might lead to timeouts and, subsequently, test failures.

Recap – special debugging commands

In this section, we learned about the Cypress special commands that can be used to provide additional debugging information. We learned that both the Cypress `debug` and `pause` commands come in handy when we want to slow down the execution of a test. We also learned that debug commands can be used as complementary tools for the Cypress tools that are provided by the test runner, such as DOM snapshots.

Summary

In this chapter, we looked at the role of debugging when it comes to executing tests. We identified aspects of the Cypress framework that make the debugging process in Cypress useful for anyone writing tests and implementing the Cypress framework. We also learned that Cypress is bundled with different tools that can be used either to achieve different purposes or the same ones. The main takeaway is that no matter what bug you encounter, Cypress will find a way for you to identify and fix it.

By completing this chapter, you have learned what page events are in Cypress, how to interpret Cypress test runner errors, how time travel works in executed tests, and how to interpret test snapshots. You also learned how to interpret console output information from Cypress and how to use the two special debugging commands that are available.

Now that we know about debugging and its impact on our tests, we can comfortably dive into the second section of this book, which will involve using Cypress with a **test-driven development** (**TDD**) approach. In the next chapter, we will develop an application by using a test-first approach, where we will write our tests before we begin developing our application. We will use these tests later on to guide us through the process of application development.

Section 2: Automated Tests with the TDD Approach

This section forms the backbone of this book and will introduce you to more advanced topics that relate to Cypress and how to use it. In this section, there will be an introduction to how we can think through an idea and use **Test-Driven Development** (**TDD**) to take our idea from the conception stage through to development. In this chapter, we will also learn about topics such as interacting with elements using Cypress, the use of aliases, and the Cypress Test Runner.

This section includes the following chapters:

6
Writing Cypress Tests Using the TDD approach

Now that we've completed *Part 1* of this book – that is, *Cypress as an End-to-End Testing Solution for Frontend Applications* – it is time to move on to *Part 2* of this book, which will focus on *Automated Tests with a TDD Approach.*

Before we can start writing Cypress tests using a **TDD** (**TDD**) approach, we need to understand how to properly write Cypress tests. This was covered in the previous chapters of this book. To excel in this topic, you will need to have an understanding of how Cypress tests work, the structure of tests, and the different ways in which Cypress tests can be used to make assertions. This background information will help you understand how to use TDD in Cypress and the advantages that come from using it in the software development life cycle. In this chapter, we will utilize a test-driven approach to write tests that will significantly contribute to an increased level of trust and confidence in our applications and software solutions.

Our focus in this chapter will be on identifying how Cypress can be utilized to help us holistically think about an application, even before we start the process of developing it. We will apply the concept of testing our application first before we start development. In doing so, we will utilize the Cypress framework as the core for our tests.

The following key topics will be covered in this chapter:

- Understanding TDD
- Writing TDD tests in Cypress
- Modifying TDD tests

Once you've worked through each of these topics, you will be ready to learn about element interaction in Cypress.

Technical requirements

To get started, we recommend that you clone this book's GitHub repository, which contains the application we will be building and all the tests that we will write in this chapter.

The GitHub repository for this chapter can be found at

`https://github.com/PacktPublishing/End-to-End-Web-Testing-with-Cypress`

The source code for this chapter can be found in the `chapter-06` directory.

We will be using the ReactJS library to develop our application.

You can run the ReactJS application by running the following commands:

- `cd chapter-6/tdd-todo-app`
- `npm install` (to install all the required dependencies)
- `npm run start` (to start the React application for testing purposes)

the following link:

Understanding TDD

TDD is a software development process that relies on requirements being turned into very specific test cases. After writing these test cases, the code is then written and checked against other test cases. The final step in the TDD process is to iterate and improve the code to make sure it adheres to the best practices required and that the test cases pass. The cycle of a TDD approach consists of the following steps:

1. Defining the functionality that needs to be implemented
2. Writing a new test
3. Running the test to check whether the test fails
4. Writing code for the test case to pass
5. Running the test against the added functionality to make sure the test passes
6. Refactoring the code
7. Repeating this process

The purpose of TDD is to visualize the end before development has started. That way, it is possible to foresee the problems or hurdles that may arise during the development process. Being able to develop a feature using the TDD approach assists in critically thinking about the solution, and also helps with scenarios that need to be tested as the application is being developed.

Let's say we are creating a login functionality; from a testing perspective, we will need to come up with all the different scenarios for the login feature. Thinking about these test scenarios will give us a clear view of what needs to take place in the development phase, making the requirements clearer when we are developing this application feature.

TDD assists in reducing the chances of scope creep since, from the onset, we can understand the goal of the project. With test cases in place, we can determine the functionality and limit the scope to only the test cases that have been written. Understanding what this feature involves allows developers to formulate how the code will be implemented. In the long run, this might lead to reduced development time.

> **Important Note**
>
> Scope creep refers to uncontrolled changes or the scope of a software development project growing after the project has begun.

Next, let's take a look at the advantages of the TDD approach.

Advantages of TDD

In this section, we will take a closer look at the benefits that come from implementing the TDD methodology in a software development life cycle.

Better project design

When developing using the TDD approach, developers need to think of the goal that the piece of code is meant to achieve. Due to this, developers will always start with the end in mind. The ability to develop a feature with a specific goal ensures that developers only write code that is needed and is necessary, which subsequently leads to the application having a clear structure.

Using TDD also ensures higher code quality as TDD strongly emphasizes the use of the **Don't Repeat Yourself** (**DRY**) principles, which discourage repetition when writing code. Due to this, by using TDD, it is possible to keep functions simple and brief, and the code base easy to understand. A cleaner and simple code base is easy to maintain and test, which is an added advantage to the developers and the code base maintainers.

> **Important Note**
>
> DRY principles are application development principles that emphasize the non-repetition of software patterns and the use of abstraction to avoid or reduce redundancy.

Detailed documentation

TDD enforces strict documentation that references the feature under development; developers need to come up with such specifications, which might well include the actions of the users. Understanding the actions and breaking down the steps into user stories helps developers implement the features and therefore develop features that are very close to the defined goal.

Developing proper documentation at the stage of writing tests also relieves other parties of the role of having to understand the features to reproduce documentation, since it was already part of the software development process.

Reduced development time

It is possible to assume that TDD takes more time when developing an application and in most cases, this is the truth. From this statement, we can assume that TDD will most likely delay the project delivery date, which is not the case.

By taking a TDD approach, it is possible to cover scenarios that would otherwise have bugs if a TDD approach was not used in development. While TDD may initially consume more time than the non-TDD approach, it significantly reduces the time it takes for developers to maintain the project and the work that has to be done to test the product and its features.

Since TDD enforces clean code, it goes without saying that even when bugs are identified, it is easier to fix them in a project that utilizes TDD than in a project that does not utilize TDD. The focus of TDD on high-quality code standards and continuous feedback makes the code base of TDD projects maintainable, which is not the case for non-TDD projects.

Cost savings

In any project, it is cheaper to find and fix a bug when it is still in development than when the bug has already made its way to production. TDD focuses on bug elimination as development takes place, which greatly reduces the chances of defects making their way through the development and testing phases of a feature. This enforces code refactoring principles and bug prevention. The TDD approach greatly saves the company's expenditure on actions that are directly related to bugs and defects being discovered in production.

Costs that come as a direct result of a defect can include direct loss of revenue, additional time and costs to fix the discovered defect, and even loss of trust by the stakeholders of the company, such as the customers. Understanding the ability of TDD to lower such costs makes the savings in a company worthwhile since developing software costs money and fixing the same software costs even more money.

Reliable solutions

TDD solutions are reliable as they undergo scrutiny before development kicks off. TDD ensures that the concept that was developed is what is achieved. This is realized by the test scenarios that are written when the functionality is still an idea and are in the form of requirements.

Without the use of TDD, it is not possible for developers to build a robust solution without thinking about how different parts of the program will interact with the new features. With TDD, however, these test cases help developers understand how new features and existing features can be integrated, and therefore have knowledge of how the application will behave once the new features have been built. This approach gives developers confidence as they know about the solution before they have started developing it.

Disadvantages of TDD

While most of the outcomes of TDD are positive and lead to productivity and great development processes, TDD can also be detrimental to teams that are not structured to use it. In this section, we will highlight the disadvantages of using TDD and why it may not be suitable for some teams.

Organizational preparedness

TDD requires organizations to be present in the process of implementing it. TDD requirements need to be defined for the organizations before the implementation takes place, so to guarantee success, organizations need to be positioned in such a way that TDD will work for them. In some cases, organizations may not have the patience to wait for all the requirements before implementation begins, and also might not be willing to sacrifice the extra time to critically walk through the requirements beforehand.

TDD is structural and requires both management and the team of developers to align by agreeing to incur costs related to planning beforehand so that they spend less on maintenance later. Not all teams might be willing to take on the approach of waiting for the benefits of TDD, which means the organization may not be willing to pay for the costs that are not currently visible.

Understanding problems

Test Driven Development focuses on building tests before implementation begins. This approach assists the team to better understand the problem and come up with solid implementation solutions. The greatest challenge with writing tests is that they cannot solve logical errors that have already been introduced in the implementation code. Tests can only identify what they are meant to test and may not be able to test things that have not been explicitly defined in the code.

With TDD, it is possible to make mistakes due to the understanding of the problem; tests might not be in a position to capture situations where the requirements were not properly understood by the designer of the solution.

Recap – understanding TDD

In this section, we learned about TDD, why we need it, and how it is utilized in the software development life cycle. We also learned about the advantages of using TDD and how it can prevent costs that arise from bugs and defects being discovered in the post-development and testing stages. We also learned about the disadvantages of utilizing TDD, some of which may arise from tests being as good as the reasoning with which they were written. It is therefore critical to understand the problem being developed in order to come up with tests for the problem at hand. In the next section, we will focus on writing TDD tests in Cypress and how this process assists in coming up with robust solutions and implementations for feature code.

Writing TDD tests in Cypress

In this section, we will focus on writing TDD tests using Cypress. Throughout this section, we will build a Todo application and apply the TDD principles. First, we need to have a design in mind so that we can write proper tests and also critically think about the features of our application. The goal of this chapter will be to create an application that will add todo items, delete todo items, show added todo items, and show the count of the added todo items. A mockup of the final application is shown in the following screenshot. Every step we follow will help us achieve the mockup we desire:

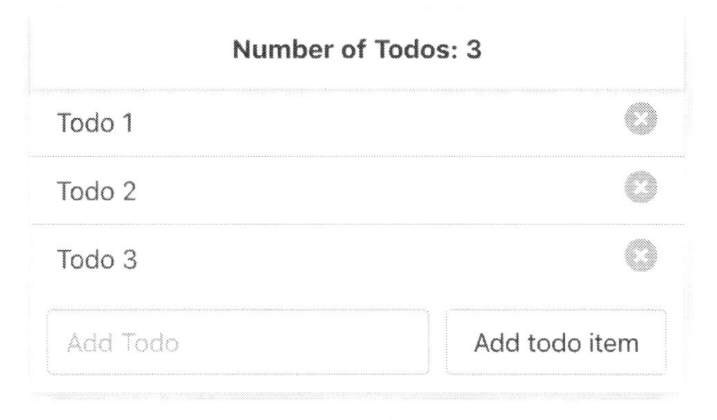

Figure 6.1 – Todo application mockup

The preceding screenshot shows a mockup of our Todo application that we will be building. We will use a TDD approach with tests written in Cypress. The application will have the following features:

- Adding new todo items
- Deleting todo items
- Viewing added todo items
- Viewing a count of added todo items

These features make up the requirements of our todo application. Throughout this chapter, we will be referencing these features as requirements as we develop our tests and implement our application.

Setting up the application

To avoid any further complexity in this section, we will not focus on how we will build the application but on how we will be implementing the tests as we build the application. For background context, the application we will be building will be using the ReactJS library, which is written in JavaScript.

Having understood what our application looks like, we will take a step-by-step approach to writing our tests before we begin the process of developing our application. As we mentioned previously, we have written the application features that we will be building toward. We will start by writing TDD tests so that we can add new todo items.

Adding new todo items

The first TDD tests that we will focus on are tests that will be responsible for checking that new todo items have been added to our todo list. To follow these steps, navigate to the `tests` directory that you cloned from GitHub with the following command:

```
cd chapter-6/tdd-todo-app/integration/todo-v1.spec.js
```

The preceding command will navigate you to the TDD `tests` directory that we will be using in this chapter. The tests located in this file are the first versions of the tests that we will write in our TDD process. Later, we will modify them so that they suit the final application features that we will add.

> **Important Note**
>
> When writing TDD tests for our Todo application, note that the Cypress directory is located inside the test application. This ensures that we keep track of and identify Cypress tests that belong to the application being developed.

The following code snippet is a test that checks that we can add a new todo item to our application, which is one of the requirements for our application:

```
it('can create and display new todo', () => {
    cy.get('[data-testid="todo-item-input"]')
      .type('New todo');
    cy.get('[data-testid="add-todo-button"]')
      .click();
    cy.contains('New Todo');
});
```

In the preceding code snippet, we wrote a TDD test to check that after the feature is complete, we can add our todo item and check that the added item exists. Note that at this stage, the feature for adding todo items has not been built yet. If we run this code snippet in Cypress, it should automatically fail. To verify this, we can run the following command to run the Cypress tests:

```
npm run cypress:open
```

The following screenshot shows a failing TDD test for creating and displaying a new todo item:

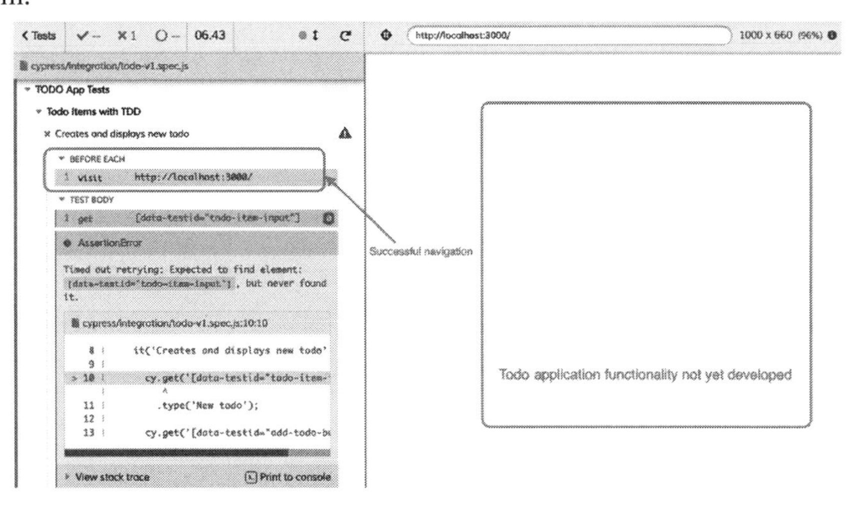

Figure 6.2 – Running a TDD test on Cypress

In the preceding screenshot, we are executing the test to check whether or not it fails and whether Cypress can execute it. In this test, Cypress tried to execute the test against the locally running Todo application running on port `3000`. The test failed because Cypress could not find the input element that is responsible for adding todo items to the todo list. From the preceding screenshot, we can verify that the application successfully navigated to our application running in localhost. To continue building on this feature and ensuring that the tests are passing, later, we will add the functionality for adding a todo item and rerun our tests again.

Deleting a Todo item

Our Todo application requirements state that we should have the ability to delete an added todo item. One of the requirements of a deleted todo item is that once it is deleted, it should no longer be visible on the todo list. To write our TDD test, we need to ensure that we actually deleted the todo item by verifying that the todo item no longer exists once it is deleted from the todo list. We will use the following code snippet to achieve the deletion feature test requirements:

```
it(can delete added todo item', () => {
        cy.get('[data-testid="todo-item-input"]')
          .type('New todo');
        cy.get('[data-testid="add-todo-button"]')
          .click();
        cy.get('[data-testid="delete-todo-1-button"]')
          .click();
        expect('[data-testid="todolist"]'
        ).not.to.contain('New Todo')
    });
```

In the preceding code block, we added a todo item and then deleted it. Later, we verified that the deleted todo item does not exist anymore and asserted that by using a Cypress assertion method. This test snippet not only checks for the proper deletion of the todo item, but also checks that after deletion takes place, the todo item will no longer be present in the DOM. As shown in the preceding screenshot, running this test with Cypress fails as our application has not been built yet.

Viewing the added todo items

As specified by our application requirements, when todo items are added, they should be visible in the todo list. The todo items that are added should be identical to the todo items in the todo list. To achieve a proper test, we need to ensure that our test covers the scenario of ensuring that an added todo item is visible on the todo list. We also need to verify that the item that has been added to the todo application is the same item that is visible on the todo list. Once again, we will curate a TDD test that will aim to cover the scenarios of being able to display our todo items. The following code block is a TDD test for displaying an added todo item:

```
it(can view added todo item', () => {
        cy.get('[data-testid="todo-item-input"]')
          .type('New todo');
        cy.get('[data-testid="add-todo-button"]')
          .click();
        expect('[data-testid="todolist"]').to.contain(
        'New Todo')
  });
```

In this code block, the TDD test will add a new todo item using the input element of the application, and then verify that the added element is present in the todo list. Having this test in place eliminates the possibility that todo items will be added and not be visible on the todo item list.

Viewing a count of the added todo items

Following the requirements of our application, we need to ensure that we can view the number of added todo items. From our mockup, which can also be found in our `chapter-06/mockups/todo-mockup.png` directory, the number of todo items should correspond to the items inside the todo list. Using the requirement for our todo app, our TDD test should test scenarios such as adding more than one todo item and checking that the number of todo items increases or decreases, depending on whether they are added or removed from our todo list.

> **Important Note**
>
> Before we write our tests, it is important to understand how Cypress understands which element to interact with, which button to click, or where to type on an input field. Cypress uses element identifiers, which uniquely identify the elements for Cypress to interact with. The unique element identifiers of elements on a web page may include unique element ID CSS selectors, XPath locators, or even custom element identifiers of our choosing, which will be in the `[data-testid="our-unique-identifier"]` format.

This test, unlike the test scenarios for adding, deleting, or viewing a todo item, will encompass multiple steps and more than one assertion. The following code block shows a TDD test for viewing the number of todo items that have been added to a todo list:

```
it('can view number of added todo items', () => {
        cy.get('[data-testid="todo-item-input"]')
          .type('New todo');
        cy.get('[data-testid="add-todo-button"]')
          .click();
        cy.get('[data-testid="todo-item-input"]')
          .type('Another todo');
        cy.get('[data-testid="add-todo-button"]')
          .click();
        expect('[data-testid="todo-item-number"]').to.eq('2')
        cy.get('[data-testid="delete-todo-1-button"]')
        .click();
        expect('[data-testid="todo-item-number"]').to.eq('1')
      });
```

This code snippet will serve as a template for the final test, which will check that the number of todo items increases and decreases as todo items are added and deleted. Here, we can see that we added two todo items, then verified that both todo items are present. After validating that both items were present in the todo list, we deleted one todo item and checked that the count of todo items decreases as the number of items decreases.

> **Important Note**
>
> When writing TDD tests, we are not very concerned about the syntax errors that may be present in the tests but rather the scenarios and test coverage. When we start modifying the tests once the features have been built, we will fix errors as we run our tests again, this time against the added functionality.

Now, it's time for a quick recap.

Recap – setting up the application

In this section, we learned about writing TDD tests and how they help shape our thinking as we develop our solutions. We covered the process of writing TDD tests for adding a todo item, viewing a todo item, deleting a todo item, and viewing the total count of todo items in the todo list. We also learned that TDD tests help us understand the process of development and that the tests are not the final tests that we will have when the features are completed. In the next section, we will look at modifying TDD tests once the features for our application have been completed.

Modifying TDD tests

In the previous section, we looked at how TDD tests are structured and the rationale through which they are developed to suit the application under development. As we mentioned earlier, we will not go into the details of how we will develop the application. Instead, we will focus on how to integrate testing into the application under development. The application being referenced here is available in this book's GitHub repository (`https://github.com/PacktPublishing/End-to-End-Web-Testing-with-Cypress/tree/master/chapter-06/`).

In this section, we will use the TDD tests that we created in the previous section. The TDD tests that we will be building on are responsible for testing the defined requirements of the application, which are as follows:

- Adding new todo items
- Deleting todo items
- Viewing added todo items
- Viewing a count of added todo items

Now that we have written the tests, we will add features to the application as we modify them. First, we will run the first test since we have already built the feature for adding a todo item. To separate the TDD tests and the final tests in our application, we will create a new test file named `todo-v2.spec.js` that we will add our final tests to. The test file is located in the `chapter-06/tdd-todo-app/integration/todo-v2.spec.js` directory.

Adding new todo items

Here, we want to verify that the test we wrote earlier to verify the addition of a new todo item actually works. To run this test, we will ensure that our application, which was built in ReactJS, is running locally. We will run our tests against the application, which is locally hosted. Once the feature for adding new todo items has been completed, our application will look as follows:

Figure 6.3 – Adding a new todo item feature

In the preceding screenshot, we can verify that our **Add todo item** feature is working since we have already added the todo item. Now that our code seems to be working okay, it is time to check whether our tests actually pass when they're run. To do this, we will use the `todo-v2.spec.js` test file, which is a modified version of `todo-v1.spec.js`.

We have modified our test from the version 1 test file located in `todo-v1.spec.js`, and have also modified the test so that it adapts to the todo item addition feature we created in our application. The new test should look as follows:

```
it('can create and displays new todo', () => {
      cy.visit('http://localhost:3000/')
      cy.get('[data-testid="todo-input-element"]')
        .type('New todo');
      cy.get('[data-testid="add-todo-button"]')
        .click();
      cy.get('[data-testid="todolist"]'
        .contains('New todo');
    });
```

Just like in our initial test, the initial scenarios to be tested do not change. We begin by navigating to the default URL of our application running locally. Then, we add a todo item using Cypress and later verify that the added todo item is what we initially added to the input element. We can clearly check the actions as they happen in the following screenshot, which shows the successful test:

Figure 6.4 – Passing the test for adding a todo item

In the preceding screenshot, we can see that Cypress navigated to the locally hosted application and added a todo, then checked to see whether the added todo was present in the todo list.

> **Important Note**
>
> We added element identifiers that are prefixed with `data-testid=*` to our application to uniquely identify elements. Element identifiers are very handy when it comes to selecting elements in a web application. By adding unique identifiers and not using the default CSS selectors for the application, even when the application selectors change, our tests will remain unaffected and will continue to run normally.

With that, we have successfully completed our first task in TDD. In this section, we achieved the following:

- Identified an application that we wanted to develop and prototyped it
- Wrote TDD tests before development started
- Developed the feature for adding a todo item to our application
- Modified the TDD tests to make them conform to our developed feature

The following screenshot shows a side-by-side comparison of both the TDD version and the final feature version of the tests for adding a new todo:

```
context('TODO App Tests', () => {
  beforeEach(() => {
    cy.visit('http://localhost:3000/')
  });
  describe('Todo Items with TDD', () => {
    it('can create and display new todo', () => {
      cy.get('[data-testid="todo-item-input"]')
        .type('New todo');
      cy.get('[data-testid="add-todo-button"]')
        .click();
      cy.contains('New Todo');
    });
VERSION 1
```

```
context('TODO App Tests', () => {
  beforeEach(() => {
    cy.visit('http://localhost:3000/')
  });
  describe('Todo Items with TDD', () => {
    it.only('can create and display new todo', () => {
      cy.get('[data-testid="todo-input-element"]')
        .type('New todo');
      cy.get('[data-testid="add-todo-button"]')
        .click();
      cy.get('[data-testid="todolist"]').contains('New todo');
    });
VERSION 2
```

Figure 6.5 – TDD test versus final feature test comparison

As you can see, the second version of the test reveals that while the test structure or objective did not change, we had to modify our test so that it suited the developed todo addition feature. The ability to identify requirements, develop a feature, and then modify the tests to run against the feature is the main goal of TDD, which we managed to achieve.

Deleting a todo item

Now, we will learn how to delete an added todo item. Regarding our requirements, a deleted todo item is removed from the list of todo items and is not visible once the delete button for the todo item is clicked. Again, we will not focus on the process of developing the feature but on the tests for this feature. In the following screenshot, we can see the delete button for every new todo item that is added:

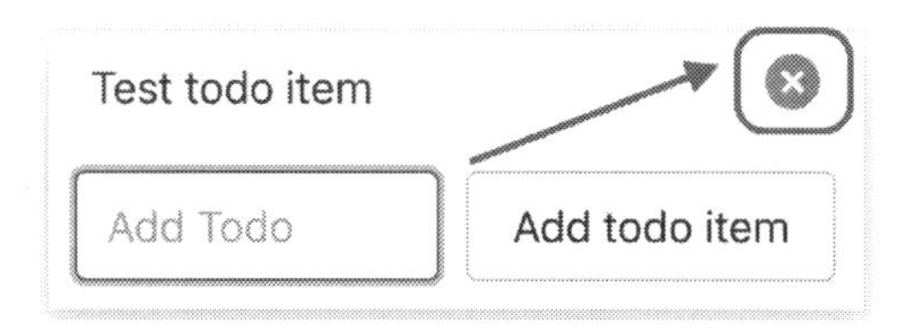

Figure 6.6 – Delete todo item feature

The icon that's highlighted in red is the delete icon that appears for every todo item. If the delete button is clicked, the added todo item will disappear from our todo list, as described in our requirements. To validate that the feature works according to how we had envisioned it, we will now modify our TDD test for the delete feature and run the test against this feature. The following code block is a test that deletes a todo item that has already been added to the todo list:

```
it('can delete an added todo item', () => {
        cy.visit('http://localhost:3000/')
        cy.get('[data-testid="todo-input-element"]')
```

```
            .type('New todo');
        cy.get('[data-testid="add-todo-button"]')
            .click();
        cy.get('[data-testid="delete-todo-0-button"]')
            .click();
        expect('[data-testid="todolist"]'
            .not.to.contain('New todo')
    });
```

This code block shows the modified TDD test for confirming that once a todo item has been deleted, it is no longer present in the todo items list. We also had to make some minor modifications to the test from the initial TDD test that we had written, so that all the selectors and actions matched the feature that has been developed. Looking at the following Cypress screenshot, we can see that our test passes and that the added todo item is deleted, as we expected:

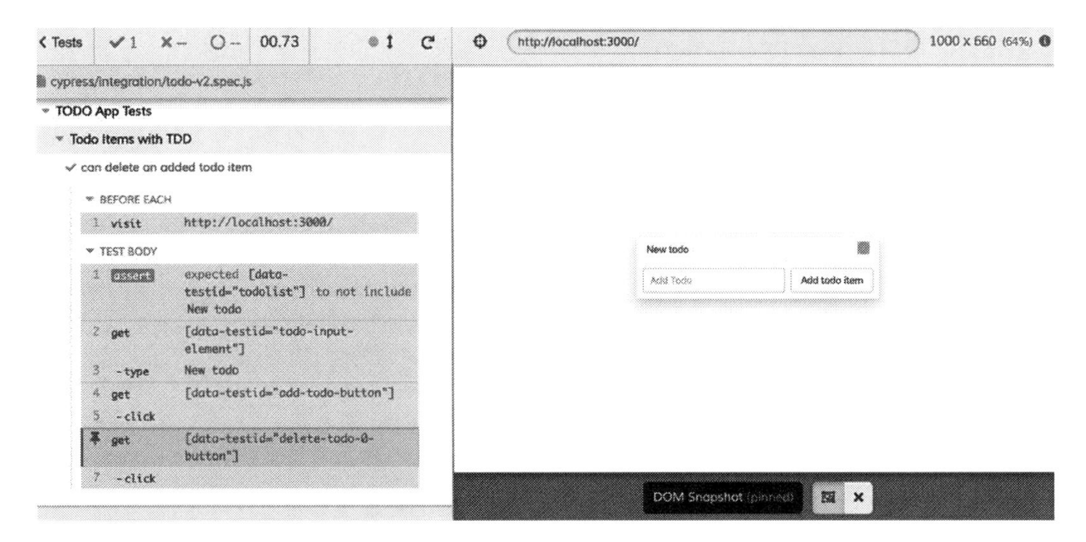

Figure 6.7 – Deleting an added todo item

Here, the Cypress snapshot feature helps us visualize the process of Cypress clicking on the delete button of the newly added todo item. We have also written an assertion to verify that the deleted todo does not exist on the todo list once it has been deleted. Our test has passed, which means that we have used TDD to add a todo item to a todo list and have also deleted this todo item and tested that it does not exist in our todo list. In our next test, we will focus on viewing added todo items.

Viewing added todo items

Part of the requirements for our application includes viewing added todo items in the todo list. While adding todo items, we have been able to see this feature in action but have not tested it. To verify this feature, we will add a new todo item and check whether the created todo item appears on the todo list. The following code block is a test that checks whether the added todo items are visible on the application that we have created:

```
it('can view added todo items', () => {
        cy.visit('http://localhost:3000/')
        cy.get('[data-testid="todo-input-element"]')
        .type('New todo, {enter}')
        cy.get('[data-testid="todo-input-element"]')
        .type('Another todo, {enter}')
        cy.get('[data-testid="todolist"]').contains(
        'New todo');
        cy.get('[data-testid="todolist"]'
        .contains('Another todo');
    });
```

Here, we have modified our TDD test. Rather than only checking whether we can view a single todo item, we have added two items and added an assertion to check that both items exist in the todo list. We will run our tests in Cypress and use the application preview to verify that both Todo items exist, as shown in the following screenshot:

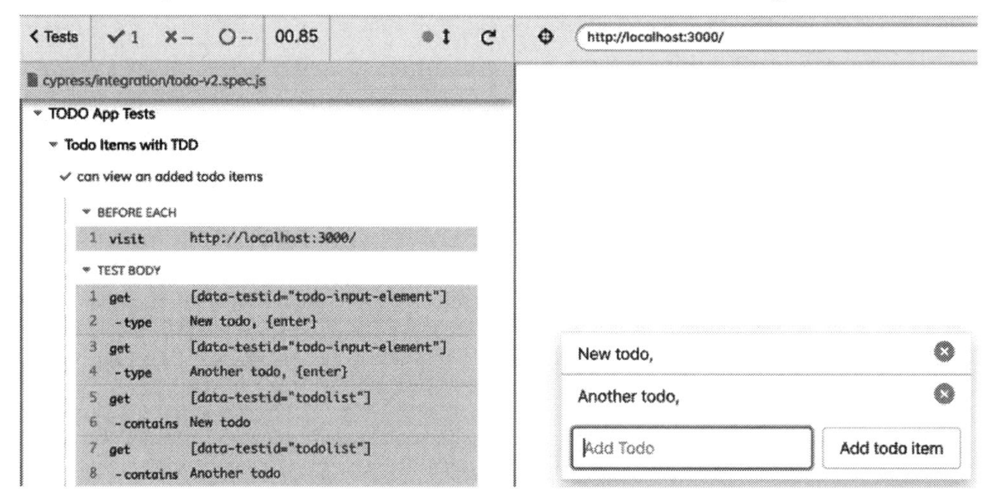

Figure 6.8 – Viewing added todo items

Hurray! Our test passes!

This screenshot shows that our requirement of having a feature that adds a todo item was correctly built, and that our test requirements for viewing todo items in our todo list were also met. Here, we have achieved our goal of viewing our todo items feature. We have also used TDD to check for scenarios that needed to be tested when viewing our todo items.

Viewing the count of added todo items

Now that we have modified our TDD tests for adding a todo item, deleting a todo item, and viewing todo items in our todo list, we also want to add a feature that checks the number of todo items that have been added. The feature for viewing the count of our added todo items is shown in the following screenshot:

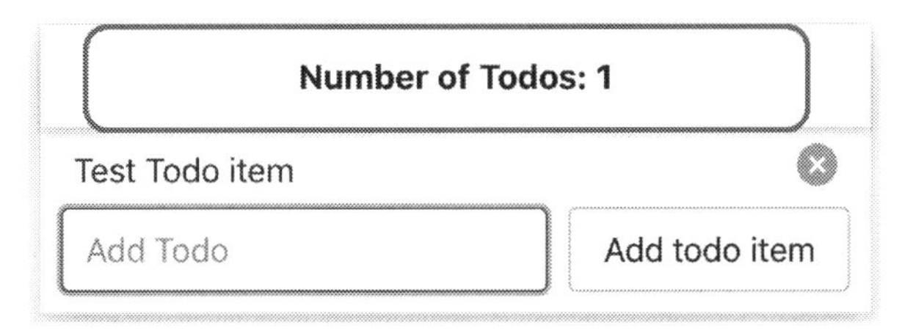

Figure 6.9 – Viewing the count of added todo items

This feature displays the number of todo items that are currently available in our todo list. The count of todo items will increase as more todo items are added and decrease when todo items are deleted from the list. Here, we will use our TDD test that we wrote for this feature and modify it so that it can be used by our application. In our test, we will focus on adding and deleting todo items and validating that on addition and deletion, the number of todo items changes accordingly. The following code block shows different assertions that check whether the feature works as it should, as per our requirements:

```
it('can view number of added todo items', () => {
      cy.visit('http://localhost:3000/')
      cy.get('[data-testid="todo-input-element"]')
      .type('New todo, {enter}')
      cy.get('[data-testid="todo-input-element"]')
      .type('Another todo, {enter}')
      cy.get('[data-testid="todo-item-number"]')
      .should(($header) => {
        expect($header.get(0).innerText).to.contain('2')
      })
      cy.get('[data-testid="delete-todo-1-button"]')
      .click();
```

```
    cy.get('[data-testid="todo-item-number"]')
   .should(($header) => {
       expect($header.get(0).innerText).to.contain('1')
    })
  });
```

The preceding code snippet shows us adding new todo items, verifying that an item from the list was deleted, and that the count remains consistent through the different state changes of the application. Here, we have modified our initial TDD tests and have been able to use them to test whether we can actually increment or decrement the count of the todo items available. By running the same test on Cypress, we can verify that Cypress is happy and that we have a remaining todo item that was not deleted, as shown in the following screenshot:

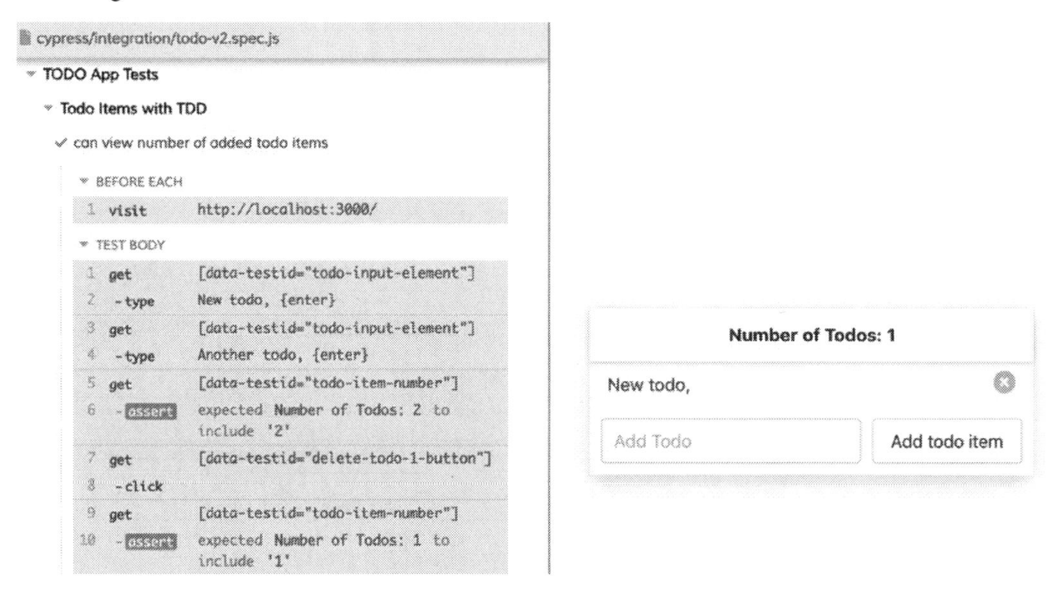

Figure 6.10 – Testing the todo count

From the preceding screenshot, we can verify that as the state of the application changes due to actions such as adding and deleting todo items, the count increases or decreases accordingly.

Recap – modifying TDD tests

In this section, we learned how to modify TDD tests once features have been developed to make them conform to how our application has been built. We also learned how Cypress uniquely identifies what elements to interact with when our tests are running. Finally, we learned how to transform already written TDD tests into test features that have been developed for our application.

Summary

In this chapter, we understood how the process of TDD works and the importance of embracing TDD in any team, and looked at the advantages and disadvantages of TDD. We also explored how TDD can be applied to a practical application. By doing this, we created requirements for a Todo application that had not been built yet. Before developing the application, we wrote TDD tests for the features we thought were important, and then used these requirements and TDD tests to develop our features. Once we'd finished developing our features, we modified our first TDD versions of the tests so that they work for our developed features, hence completing the process of showcasing how to utilize TDD in a practical application.

Now, you should understand what TDD is, how to write TDD tests, and how to modify and use TDD tests in a real-world application so that they conform to the developed application.

Now that we know about TDD and how to implement it in our projects, we will focus on how to interact with the different elements of the Cypress DOM in the next chapter.

7

Understanding Element Interaction in Cypress

Before we get started with how Cypress interacts with elements when running tests, it would be good to have a solid idea of the principles that make up Cypress, how it works, different Cypress commands, and even practical examples of the usage of Cypress. To fully understand this chapter, you will need to have followed the previous chapters, which will have set you up for success in your learning journey.

In this chapter, we will cover how Cypress interacts with elements and how it responds to different states of an element during interaction. We will also cover the fundamentals of how Cypress determines whether an element is ready for interaction or not through built-in mechanisms in Cypress commands.

We will cover the following key topics in this chapter:

- Understanding actionability
- Forcing actionability

Once you've worked through each of these topics, you will have the knowledge required to understand how Cypress interprets tests as they are executed and how it interprets errors that have occurred while executing tests.

Technical requirements

To get started, we recommend that you clone the repository that contains the source code and all the tests that we will write in this chapter from GitHub.

The GitHub repository for this chapter can be found at the following site:

`https://github.com/PacktPublishing/End-to-End-Web-Testing-with-Cypress`

The source code for this chapter can be found in the `chapter-07` directory.

Understanding actionability

Now that we know what Cypress commands are, and where and when to use them, we need to understand the thought and operation process of Cypress when executing tests. In this section, we will cover how Cypress interacts with commands, how it ensures that elements are visible and actionable, and even how animation in elements is handled. We will also cover how Cypress determines **actionability** before any command is completed.

Actionability is the ability of Cypress to perform an action on a specific element in the **Document Object Model (DOM)**. Cypress has commands whose sole intention is to interact with DOM elements. The commands act "as a user" and simulate interaction with the user interface of an application. Cypress events are responsible for the behavior of the commands as it sends the events to the browser, making it seem like user interaction on the application's user interface.

The following are some commands in Cypress that directly interact with the DOM; for the actions to be completed, the DOM elements have to be actionable. These commands come with built-in Cypress mechanisms for checking the actionability of the elements that they interact with. The commands include the following:

- `cy.type()`: Types into a DOM element
- `cy.clear()`: Clears the value of a text area or an input box
- `cy.click()`: Performs a click action on a DOM element
- `cy.dbclick()`: Performs a double-click action on a DOM element
- `cy.rightclick()`: Performs a right-click action on a DOM element

- `cy.select()`: Selects an `<option>` choice from a `<select>` dropdown
- `cy.trigger()`: Performs a trigger event on an element on the DOM
- `cy.check()`: Checks radios and checkboxes on the DOM
- `cy.uncheck()`: Unchecks radios and checkboxes on the DOM

> **Important note**
> The `cy.rightclick()` command will not open the browser menus, but instead will check the behavior of your elements in relation to the browser's **context menu**.

Before any of the preceding commands can be run, Cypress takes actions to ensure that the DOM is ready to receive the action. For any of the commands to take place, Cypress performs its own checks to verify that the conditions are right for the commands to be performed on the DOM elements.

All the checks take place within a specified time that can be configured through the **defaultCommandTimeout** configuration option, which can be modified in the `cypress.json` file. The following are the actions taken by Cypress to check for DOM element readiness:

- **Visibility**: Scrolls the element to view
- **Disability**: Ensures that the element is not hidden
- **Detached**: Checks that element has not been removed from the DOM
- **Readonly**: Checks that an element is not in a read-only state
- **Animations**: Checks that animations have completed
- **Covering**: Checks that an element is not being covered by a parent element
- **Scrolling**: Checks for the scrolling of elements covered by elements with fixed positions
- **Coordinates**: Checks that the event is fired at the desired coordinates

To better understand how Cypress interprets responses from the DOM and how it determines actionability, we will go through these listed actions and describe how Cypress checks the state through every single action when an actionable command is executed.

Visibility

Cypress uses different factors to determine whether an element is visible or not. The default way that Cypress determines the visibility of an element is by checking the **Cascading Style Sheets** (**CSS**) properties of that element. The CSS properties of any element define how the element behaves and if, by default, the CSS properties are defined in a way that means the element is hidden, Cypress will automatically know that the element is not visible due to its properties.

Cypress considers an element to be hidden if any of the following conditions are met:

- The CSS `width` and `height` of an element are `0`.
- The element or its ancestors have a `visibility: hidden` CSS property.
- The element or its ancestors have a `display: none` CSS property.
- The element has a `position: fixed` CSS property and it is covered up or not present on the screen.

Additionally, Cypress uses the `hidden overflow` CSS property to determine whether an element is hidden or not during the execution of tests. The following additional instances are some that Cypress uses to determine whether an element is hidden or not:

- Ancestors have hidden overflow and `width` or `height` values of `0`, and there is an element between the ancestor and the element that has a CSS property of `position: absolute`.
- Ancestors have hidden overflow and the element has a CSS property of `position: relative` and is positioned outside the ancestor's bounds.

> **Important note**
>
> Hidden overflow means that the CSS property can be any of the following overflows: `hidden`, `overflow: auto`, `overflow: scroll`, `overflow-x: hidden`, or `overflow-y: hidden`.

All of the following calculations of transformations and translations are handled by Cypress, and if by any chance Cypress does not find that the element is visible, the test will fail with an error saying that visibility is hidden for the element that Cypress is trying to interact with.

Disability

When checking for actionability, Cypress also checks whether an element is disabled or not. When an element has the `disabled: true` CSS property, Cypress cannot interact with it as no action can be performed on an element when it is disabled on the DOM. When Cypress encounters a disabled element and needs to perform an action on the element, it will return an error describing the state of the disabled element and why it is not able to interact with the element through Cypress actionable commands.

Detached

Detached elements are elements that have been removed from the DOM but are still present in the memory because of the JavaScript. Most applications work by removing elements from the DOM and inserting other elements in the DOM, hence constantly detaching and attaching elements in the DOM. When evaluating an element for actionability, Cypress checks that an element is not detached before any actionable command is run on an element. In the event that Cypress encounters a detached element, it throws an error before the actionable command is executed by Cypress on the tests.

It is important to note that Cypress will only search for an element in the DOM and will not check whether a detached element exists in the memory or not.

Readonly

Readonly elements are disabled for viewing only and cannot accept new content or editing. Cypress checks for the `readonly` CSS property in the `.type()` command; if the `readonly` CSS property is encountered, the test will fail with an error.

Animations

Cypress has built-in mechanisms that determine whether animations are present in an element. When evaluating whether an element is actionable, Cypress waits for the animation to complete before interaction with the element begins.

For Cypress to determine whether an element in a test is animating, it has to use a sample of the last coordinates of the element and then apply its algorithms to calculate the slope.

> **Important note**
>
> The slope is calculated by picking two different points and recording their coordinates. Differences between the y-coordinates and the x-coordinates are then recorded. Division of the difference in the y-coordinates and the x-coordinates is then carried out to determine the slope of the element.

The animation of an element and the slope is determined by checking the current and previous positions of that element. Cypress comes with an in-built animation threshold that checks for the distance in pixels that an element must exceed to be considered to be animating. You can configure this in the `cypress.json` file and change the default values as shown in the following code block:

```
{
"animationDistanceThreshold": 10
}
```

When this value is changed, either by increasing it or decreasing it, Cypress will change its sensitivity and behavior of determining whether an element is animating or not. A higher animation threshold means that Cypress will reduce its sensitivity when it comes to detecting the changed distance of the pixels while a lower animation threshold will mean more sensitivity of Cypress when detecting elements that are animating.

It is also possible to turn off animations when running tests. To do this, we need to configure our `cypress.json` configuration file to ignore animations and continue with the execution of our commands. The following can be achieved with the configuration in this code block:

```
{
"waitForAnimations": false
}
```

When we have specified that our tests should not wait for animations, as shown here, our tests will ignore animations and will execute as if the animations are not present. This configuration can, however, be changed back to the `true` value to continue executing our tests while waiting for animations to execute in the elements.

Covering

Cypress checks that an element is not covered by a parent element as part of verifying actionability before a command is issued. There are many instances where an element could be visible in the DOM but just covered by a parent element such as a modal, a popup, or a dialog box. Cypress will not allow the execution of a command if there is a parent that is covering the element.

In instances where a parent element covers an element that Cypress is supposed to carry out an action on, Cypress will throw an error, as even in real life it would be impossible for a user to interact with a covered-up element.

> **Important note**
>
> In the event that a child element is covering the element, Cypress will continue to issue the event to the child and execution continues without any problem.

In the following code block, we have a `button` element that is partially or fully covered up by a `span` element, which will be clicked instead of the `button` element itself:

```
<button>
   <span> Submit </span>
</button>
```

In this code block, although the `span` element covers the `button` element, Cypress will issue the command to the child `span` element, which will trigger a click event to our `button` element without encountering errors.

Scrolling

Cypress performs scrolling on the elements and has this behavior enabled by default in the actionable commands specified at the beginning of this section. By default, before interaction with an element, Cypress scrolls to the position of that element and ensures that it is in view.

> **Tip**
>
> Commands such as `cy.get()` or `cy.find()` do not have the Cypress scroll-into-view mechanism built into them as actionable commands in Cypress do.

Scrolling in Cypress is enabled by an algorithm that first tries to determine whether an element is visible on the DOM. It then uses coordinates to navigate to the actual element by calculating coordinates from the present element to the desired location of the element being acted upon by Cypress.

The Cypress scroll algorithm continually scrolls until an element becomes visible or until an element is no longer being covered up by other elements. The algorithm does a good job of ensuring that most elements on the DOM can be scrolled to and interacted with when they are in view.

Coordinates

After Cypress has completed the verification process of checking whether the elements are actionable or not, by default it fires events to the center of the element. Cypress provides a mechanism to override the default position of firing the events and the behavior can be customized for most commands.

The following code block shows changing the firing behavior of a click event on a button:

```
it('can mark a todo as completed - with changed hitbox
position', () => {
cy.visit('http://todomvc.com/examples/react/#/')
        cy.get(".new-todo").type("New Todo {Enter}");
        cy.get(".new-todo").type("Another New Todo {Enter}");
        cy.get('.todo-list>li:nth-child(1)').find(
        '.toggle').click({ position: 'topLeft' });
    });
```

In this code block, we navigate to our Todo application and add two todo items, then mark one of the todo items as completed. When marking our first todo item as complete, we changed the position of the click and instructed Cypress to click on the `topLeft` position instead of the default `center` position. The following screenshot shows the **event hitbox** of the `click` command on the top-left part of the clicked todo item action:

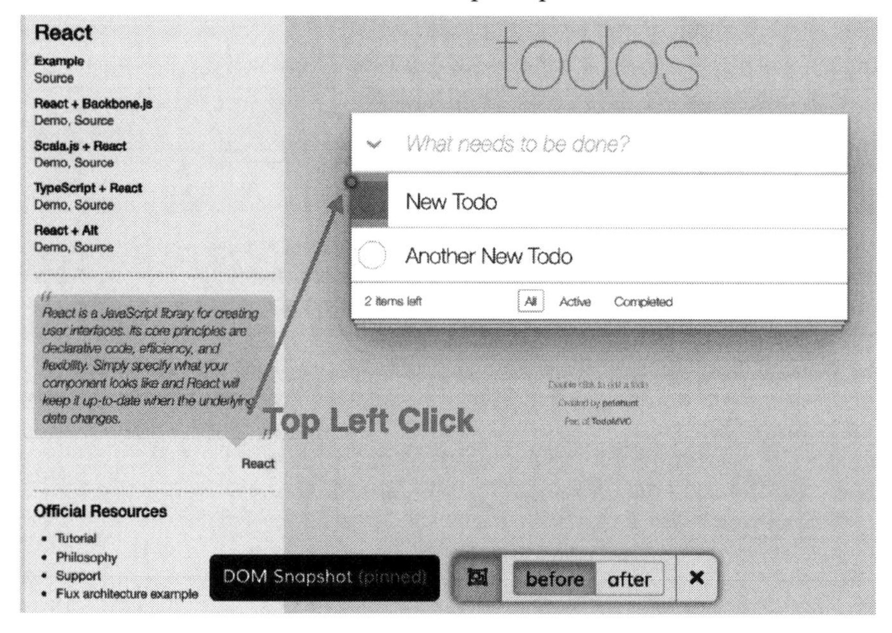

Figure 7.1 – Changing the coordinates of a Cypress click position

> **Important note**
>
> An event hitbox is a highlight that pops up on the pinned Cypress snapshots to show that the test interacted with the element. An event hitbox can be triggered by Cypress events such as the `.click()` method.

As *Figure 7.1* illustrates, Cypress has the ability to calculate the coordinates of an element and determine the exact coordinates of where to click an element. In addition, when the coordinates of the firing behavior have changed, Cypress records them on the command log of the Cypress test runner. We can further check the console for the coordinates that Cypress prints after executing the top-left click on the element. The following figure shows printed coordinates of the `click` event of the first completed todo item:

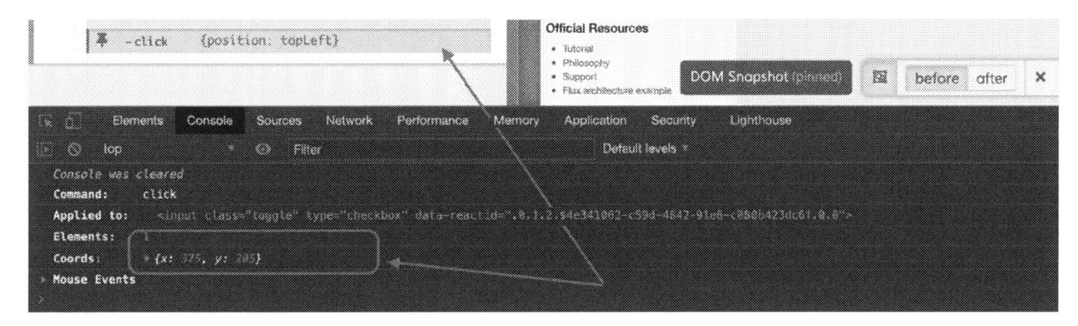

Figure 7.2 – New click position coordinates

The coordinates shown in the screenshot are the new `.click()` command coordinates that we have instructed Cypress to use instead of the default commands that come with the actionable commands.

Recap – understanding actionability

In this section, we learned about how Cypress determines the actionability of elements and how it evaluates different elements for conditions such as visibility, disability, detached modes, animations, scroll properties, coordinates, and even `readonly` properties. We also learned how Cypress calculates animations in elements and how we can increase the animation threshold to reduce the sensitivity of Cypress detecting animations.

In the next section, we will learn how we can force Cypress to continue performing actions even when the actionability checks fail for an element and when it is safe to perform the forced actions on elements.

Forcing actionability

Having understood what actionability is, and the checks that are required by Cypress to determine whether an element is actionable or not, it is also important to know how we can override mechanisms set in place by Cypress to check for actionability. In this section, we will focus on performing actions and commands even when the elements do not pass the actionability checks that Cypress enforces for the actionable commands. We will also learn how to safely implement override mechanisms for some elements and tests.

Overriding Cypress actionability checks

Actionability is very useful in Cypress tests as it helps us to find situations where users may not be able to interact with our application elements. At times, though, the actionability checks can get in the way of proper testing, which leads us to our next mission: overriding the safety checks.

In some tests, "acting like a user" may not be worth it as, at the end of the day, the goal is to write meaningful tests that can prevent bugs and defects in an automated manner. Instances such as nested navigation structures and interfaces may lead to complicated tests that can just be made possible by eliminating the nested navigation structures and instead directly interacting with the elements that we want.

To override the Cypress actionability checks, we can pass the `{force: true}` parameter option to the Cypress actionable commands. The option will instruct Cypress to override all the checks that check for actionability and instead proceed with the default actions. The following code block is a test to mark all the todo items as completed using a `toggle-all` button in our Todo application:

```
it('can mark all todo as completed - with no forced toggle
option (Failure)', () => {
        cy.get(".new-todo").type("New Todo {Enter}");
        cy.get(".new-todo").type("Another New Todo {Enter}");
        cy.get('.todo-list>li:nth-child(1)').find(
        '.toggle').click();
        cy.get('#toggle-all').click();
    });
```

When this test runs, it will fail, as trying to toggle the first element and mark it as complete will lead to a test failure and an error as it is already marked as complete. The following screenshot shows Cypress actionability in play, where the test failed as a todo it could not be marked as complete due to it being covered by another element:

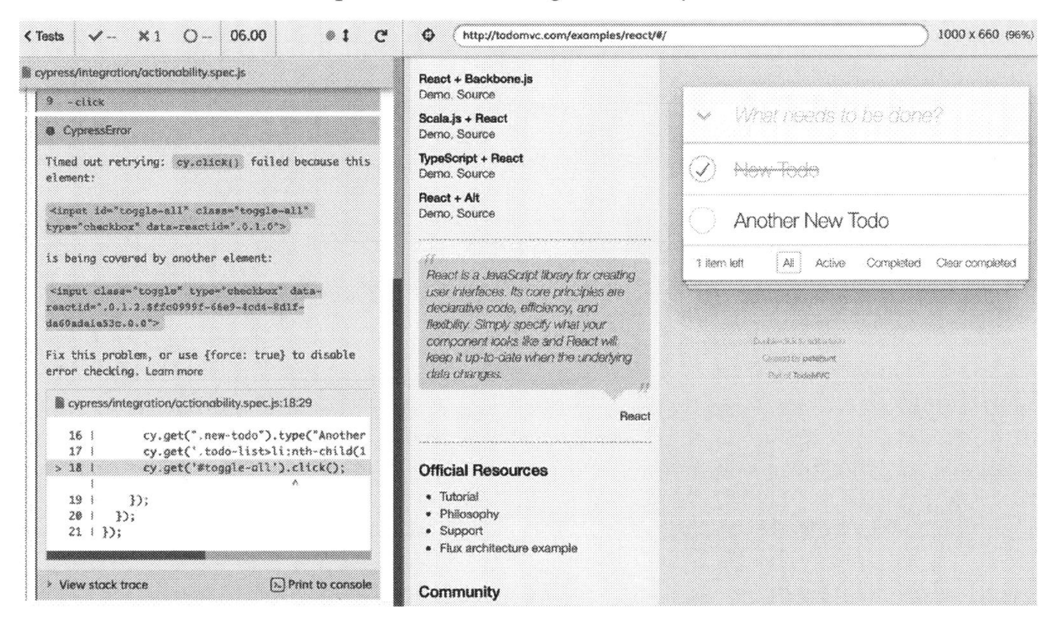

Figure 7.3 – Failed tests with Cypress actionability checks

On further investigation, from *Figure 7.3*, we can verify that the first item could not be toggled as complete as it was already complete, which led to the failure. We can override this test behavior by telling Cypress to ignore the actionability checks before toggling all the todo items to complete, as shown in the following code block:

```
it('can mark all todo as completed - with forced toggle option
(Success)', () => {
        cy.get(".new-todo").type("New Todo {Enter}");
        cy.get(".new-todo").type("Another New Todo {Enter}");
        cy.get('.todo-list>li:nth-child(1)').find(
        '.toggle').click();
        cy.get('#toggle-all').click({force: true});
    });
```

On running the test shown in the code block, it passes as we have prevented Cypress from checking whether the element that we need to click is covered by another element or not. The following screenshot shows the code running and the successful test of marking both todo items as completed by clicking the toggle-all drop-down button:

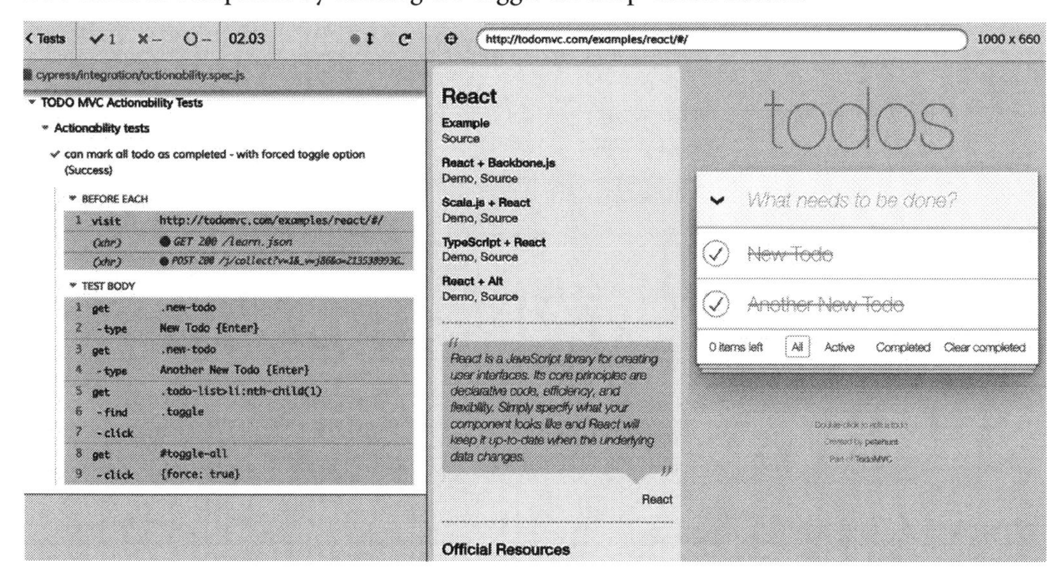

Figure 7.4 – Passed test with the override of the Cypress actionability checks

In *Figure 7.4*, Cypress ignored the checks associated with the actionability of the items and instead proceeded with the default action, which in our case was to toggle both todo items and mark them as complete. We achieved the override by passing the `{force: true}` option to the `click` command of the toggle button.

When a Cypress event is forced to happen with a forced option, Cypress does the following:

- Continues to perform all the default actions
- Forcibly fires the event at the element

However, Cypress will not do the following:

- Ensure that the element is visible
- Scroll the element to view
- Ensure that the element is not disabled

- Ensure that the element is not detached
- Ensure that the element is not animating
- Ensure that the element is not covered
- Ensure that the element is not readonly
- Fire the event at the descendant element

> **Important note**
>
> Forcing actionability is useful especially when you do not need to go through the pain of automating steps that are not worth the time it will take to automate them; however, at times, it is not the best solution to the problem at hand. Most of the issues that we face when we are forcing actionability can be addressed by writing better application code and ensuring the proper alignment of items such that no element is blocking another. We can also utilize Cypress to overcome situations such as animations as we can wait for the animations to stop running and then execute our tests once we are sure that the page animations have been completed.

When actionability is forced on a command, Cypress forgoes its role of ensuring that the right conditions are met before any action can be performed on an element and instead just performs the issued condition on the test.

Recap – forcing actionability

In this section, we have learned that it is possible to force actionability on an element, and this is achieved by passing in a `{force: true}` parameter to the actionable command being issued on an element. We have also seen that there is a significant difference when we force a command to be executed in Cypress as exemplified by the test of toggling our todo items as complete. In this section, we also understood when it is important to override Cypress actionability and how it can potentially reduce test complexity.

Summary

In this chapter, we have learned how Cypress enforces actionability for elements by ensuring that they are in the correct state before commands are performed on the elements. We learned that Cypress checks for visibility, disability, DOM detachment, `readonly` modes, animations, covering, scrolling, and element coordinates before it performs any action on an element. We also went through how Cypress calculates the animation of elements and even how it changes the coordinates when actions are being performed on elements. We also learned that it is possible to override the default checks that Cypress puts in place by forcing actionability in our tests.

Having completed this chapter, I believe you have the skills needed to understand how Cypress determines actionability for elements and also how we can override actionability in our tests to reduce complexity. In the next chapter, we will look at using variables and aliases, and we will dive into reusing variables and aliases that we define in our tests more than once.

8 Understanding Variables and Aliases in Cypress

Before we get started on how variables and aliases work in Cypress, it is important to understand what we covered in the previous chapters on how to write tests in Cypress, how to configure tests, and even how to use Cypress to write applications in the proper way by following a test-driven development approach. The background information provided in the previous chapters of this book will give you a good grounding as we dive into how variables and aliases work. By exploring what variables and aliases are, we will understand how we can create references in Cypress, which will ease our test writing process and the complexity of our tests. Understanding how to use variables and aliases will not only make you write better tests but also write tests that are easy to read and maintain.

In this chapter, we will focus on writing asynchronous commands to make use of the variables and aliases that Cypress comes bundled with. We will also understand how we can simplify our tests by using aliases and how we can utilize the aliases and the variables we create in different areas of our tests such as references to elements, routes, and requests.

We will cover the following key topics in this chapter:

- Understanding Cypress variables
- Understanding Cypress aliases

Once you've worked through each of these topics, you will have a full understanding of how to utilize aliases and variables in your Cypress tests.

Technical requirements

To get started, we recommend that you clone the repository containing the source code and all the tests that we will write in this chapter from GitHub.

The GitHub repository for this chapter can be found at `https://github.com/PacktPublishing/End-to-End-Web-Testing-with-Cypress`.

The source code for this chapter can be found in the `chapter-08` directory.

Understanding Cypress variables

This section will focus on what variables are in Cypress, how they are used in tests, and their roles in tests, especially in the reduction of test complexity. We will also explore different areas where we can use Cypress variables to add readability to our tests. By the end of this section, you will be able to write tests using variables and also understand where variables should be used when writing your tests.

To better understand how variables in Cypress work, it is important to understand how Cypress executes its commands. The following code block is a test that first selects a button and then selects an input element, then later clicks the button:

```
it('carries out asynchronous events', () => {
    const button = cy.get('#submit-button');
    const username = cy.get('#username-input');

    button.click()
});
```

The preceding code block illustrates a test that should first identify a button, then next identify a username input, and finally, click the button. However, the test and execution will not happen in the way that we would normally assume. In our assumptions, we might think that the first command will execute and return the results before the second command runs, then the third command will be the last to execute. Cypress utilizes JavaScript **asynchronous APIs**, which control how commands are executed in Cypress tests.

> **Important note**
> The asynchronous APIs are implemented such that they provide the responses of commands or requests as they are received, and do not necessarily wait for one particular request to get a response before handling other requests. The APIs instead return the first response that was received and continue the execution of the responses that have not yet been received. The non-blocking mechanism of making requests and receiving responses ensures that different requests can be made at the same time, therefore making our application appear multi-threaded, while in reality, it is single-threaded in nature.

In the preceding code block, Cypress executes the commands in an asynchronous order where the responses are not necessarily returned in the order in which the requests are made in our test. We can, however, force Cypress to execute our tests as we desire, and we will cover this in the next section as we explore **closures** in Cypress.

Closures

Closures are created when Cypress bundles together test functions and references to the surrounding state of the functions. Closures are a JavaScript concept from which Cypress borrows heavily. A test closure in Cypress would therefore have access to the external scope of our test and also have access to its internal scope, which will be created by the test function. We refer to the local functional scope of the test as the **lexical environment**, as is the case in JavaScript functions. In the following code block, we can see what closures are in Cypress and how variables are utilized in the closure:

```
describe('Closures', () => {
    it('creates a closure', () => {
       // { This is the external environment for the test }
      cy.get('#submit-button').then(($submitBtn) => {
       // $submitBtn is the Object of the yielded cy.get()
       // response
       // { This is the lexical environment for the test }
```

```
        })
        // Code written here will not execute until .then()
        //finishes execution
    })
});
```

The `$submitBtn` variable is created to access the response gotten from the `cy.get('#submit-button')` command. Using the variable that we just created in the test, we can access the value that was returned and interact with it, just like in a normal function. In this test, we have created a test closure function using the `$submitBtn` variable. The `.then()` function creates a **callback function** that enables us to nest other commands within the code block. The advantage of closures is that we can control how our tests execute commands. In our test, we can wait until all nested commands inside the `.then()` method execute before running any other commands in our test. The execution behavior is further described by our comments in the test code.

> **Important note**
>
> Callback functions are functions passed inside other functions as arguments and are then invoked inside the outer function to complete an action. When commands inside our `.then()` function complete running, other commands outside the function will proceed with their execution routine.

In the following code block, we will explore how to write a test by using variables and ensuring that the code within the closure is executed first before any other code outside and after the closure begins execution. The test will add two to-do items, but before the addition of the second to-do item, we will use a closure to verify that the code within the closure was executed first:

```
it('can Add todo item - (Closures)', () => {
      cy.visit('http://todomvc.com/examples/react/#/')
      cy.get(".new-todo").type("New Todo {Enter}");
      cy.get('.todo-list>li:nth-child(1)').then(($todoItem) =>
{
        // Storing our todo item Name
        const txt = $todoItem.text()
        expect(txt).to.eq('New Todo')
      });
      // This command will run after all the above commands
```

```
        // have finished their execution.
        cy.get(".new-todo").type("Another New Todo {Enter}");
    });
```

In the preceding code block, we have added a to-do item to our to-do list, but before we add our second item, we validate that the added to-do item is indeed what we created. To achieve this, we use a closure and a callback function that needs to return `true` before our execution of the next command can proceed. The following screenshot shows the execution steps of our running test:

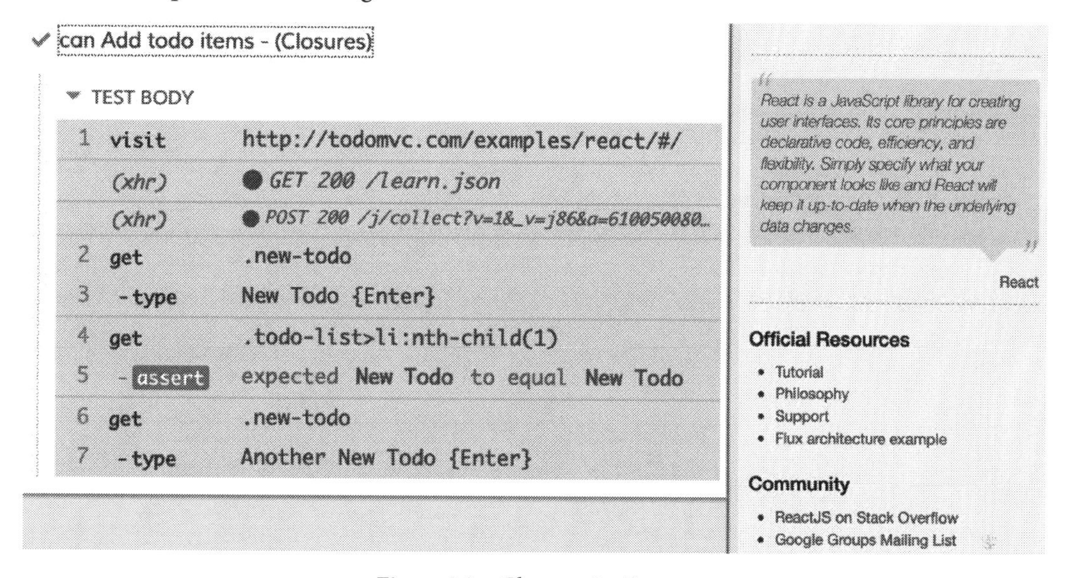

Figure 8.1 – Closures in Cypress

In *Figure 8.1*, we can see that Cypress executed the command to get the added to-do item and asserted that the added to-do item was what we had in our list before executing the last command to add a new to-do item to our to-do list.

Closures in Cypress cannot exist outside variables. To use closures, we need to utilize variables to pass the value received from our commands to the closure function, and utilizing variables is the only way to do this. In this code block, we have used a `$todoItem` variable to pass the value of the `cy.get()` command to the closure that asserts that the found to-do item is the exact item that we created.

Cypress utilizes variable scopes just as in JavaScript. In Cypress, users have the option of using `const`, `var`, and `let` identifiers to specify the scope of the variable declaration. In the following sections, we will see different scopes that can be utilized in a test.

Var

The `var` keyword is used to declare a function or a globally scoped variable. It is optional to provide the value to the variable for the purposes of initialization. A variable declared with the `var` keyword is executed before any other code is executed when it is encountered in a test function. It is possible to declare a variable in the global scope with the `var` keyword and overwrite it in the functional scope within our test function. The following code block shows a simple override of the globally scoped variable declared with the `var` keyword:

```
describe('Cypress Variables', () => {
  var a = 20;

  it('var scope context', () => {
    a = 30; // overriding global scope
    expect(a).to.eq(30) // a = 30
  });
 it('var scope context - changed context', () => {
    // Variable scope remains the same as the change affects
    // the global scope
    expect(a).to.eq(30) //a = 30
  });
});
```

In this code block, we declared an `a` variable in the global context of our tests, then later changed the global variable in our test. The newly changed variable will become the new value of our global `a` variable unless it is explicitly changed, as we did in the test. The `var` keyword therefore changes the global context of the variable, as it globally reassigns the value of the global variable.

Let

The `let` variable declaration works in the same way that `var` declared variables work, with the exception that variables defined can only be available inside the scope in which they are declared. Yes, I know that sounds confusing! In the following code block, the two tests show a difference of scope declaration while using the `let` keyword:

```
describe('Cypress Variables', () => {
  // Variable declaration
  let a = 20;

```

```
    it('let scope context', () => {
      let a = 30;
      // Local scoped variable
      expect(a).to.eq(30) // a = 30
    });
    it('let scope context - global', () => {
      // Global scoped variable
      expect(a).to.eq(30) // a = 20
    });
```

In this second test, we have a test failure as the `let` keyword will only make the changed `a` variable available to the specific test that changed it, and not to the entire global scope of our test suite, as is the case with the `var` variable declaration. In the following screenshot, we can see that the test fails as it only picks the variable declared in the `describe` block and not the one in the previous tests:

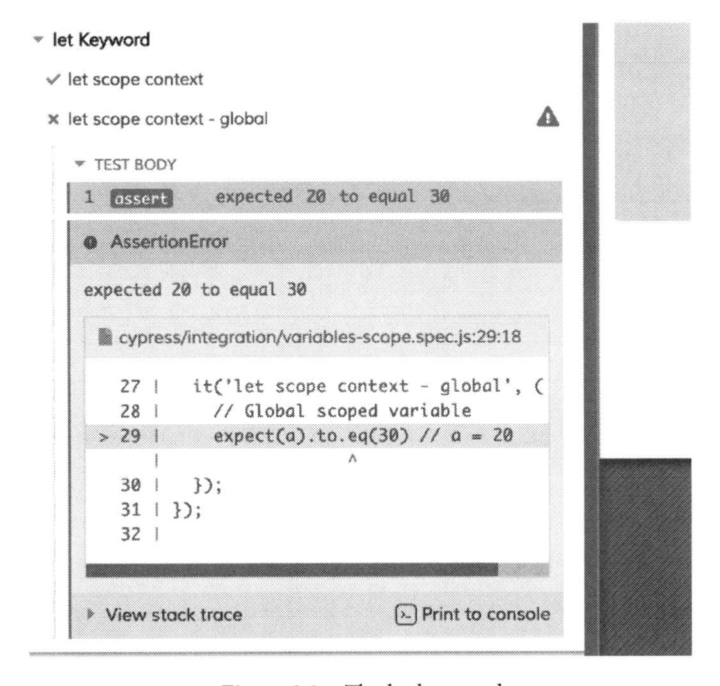

Figure 8.2 – The let keyword

As shown in *Figure 8.2*, while writing tests, it is possible to make declarations of the same variable in different tests without affecting the scope of the declared variables, as each one will belong and have its own context and not affect the global context.

Const

The `const` keyword is used to declare objects and variables that are read-only and cannot be altered or reassigned once they have been declared. Variables assigned with the `const` keyword are "final" and can only be used in the state that they are in without their values being mutated or changed. In the following code block, we are trying to reassign a variable declared with the `const` keyword, which will then result in a failure:

```
describe('const Keyword', () => {
    const a = 20;
    it('let scope context', () => {
      a = 30;
      // Fails as We cannot reassign
      // a variable declared with a const keyword
      expect(a).to.eq(30) // a = 20
    });
});
```

From this code block, given that the a variable is declared with `const`, it is immutable and therefore Cypress will fail with an error, as shown in the following screenshot:

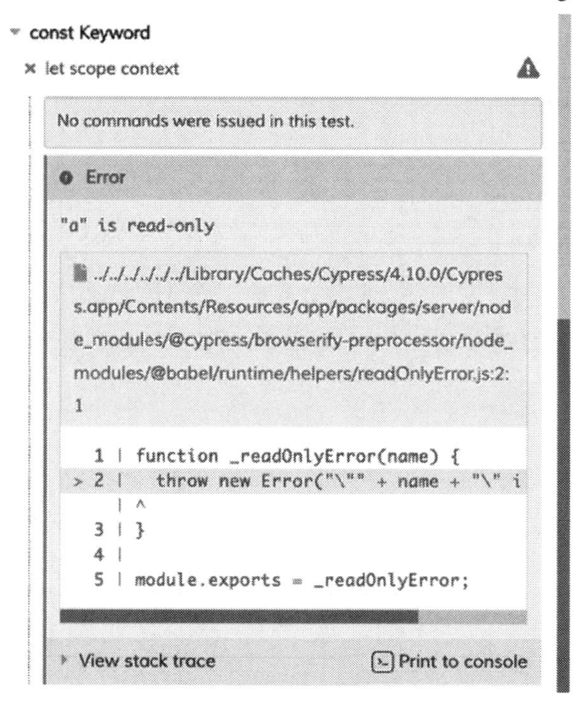

Figure 8.3 – The const keyword

Just like in JavaScript, Cypress cannot reassign a variable that has been declared with a `const` keyword. Variables declared using `const` are those that do not need to be changed during the execution of a program, neither globally or locally within the test.

Recap – Understanding Cypress variables

In this section, we learned about the utilization of variables in Cypress. We took a look at how variables are used in closures and also how they are declared with different scopes and contexts. Here, we also got to understand what variable scopes mean and how they can be used within tests. Now that we know what variables are and what they represent, we will dive into the use of aliases in Cypress tests in the next section.

Understanding Cypress aliases

Aliases are a way to prevent the usage of `.then()` callback functions in our tests. We use aliases to create references or some kind of "memory" that Cypress can refer to, hence reducing the need for us to re-declare the items all over again. A common use of aliases is to avoid using callback functions in our `before` and `beforeEach` test hooks. Aliases provide a "clean" way to access the global state of a variable without the need for calling or initializing the variable in every single test. In this section, we will learn how to properly utilize aliases in our test execution and different scenarios where using aliases is recommended.

Aliases come in handy in situations where one variable is utilized by more than one test in a test suite. The following code block shows a test where we want to verify that our to-do item does exist after we have added it to our to-do list:

```
context('TODO MVC - Aliases Tests', () => {

  let text;
  beforeEach(() => {
    cy.visit('http://todomvc.com/examples/react/#/')
    cy.get(".new-todo").type("New Todo {Enter}");
    cy.get('.todo-list>li:nth-child(1)').then(($todoItem) => {
      text = $todoItem.text()
    });
  });

  it('gets added todo item', () => {
```

```
      // todo item text is available for use
      expect(text).to.eq('New Todo')
    });
  });
```

To externally use a variable declared in the `beforeEach` or `before` hooks, we used a callback function in the code block to access the variable, and later assert that the text of the variable created by our `beforeEach` method is the same to-do item that we are expecting.

> **Important note**
>
> The structure of the code is intended for demonstration purposes only and is not recommended for use when writing your tests.

While the preceding test will definitely pass, it is an anti-pattern that Cypress aliases exist to solve. Aliases in Cypress exist to serve the following purpose in Cypress tests:

- Sharing object contexts between hooks and tests
- Accessing element references in the DOM
- Accessing route references
- Accessing request references

We will look into each of the uses of aliases and look at examples of how they can be used in the uses covered.

Sharing contexts between test hooks and tests

Aliases can provide a "clean" way of defining variables and make them accessible to the tests without using callback functions in our test hooks, as was shown in the previous code block. To create an alias, we simply add the `.as()` command to what we are sharing, and the shared elements can then be accessed from Mocha's context object using the `this.*` command. The contexts for each test are cleared after the test runs and so are the properties that our tests create in the different test hooks. The following code block shows the same test as the previous one to check whether a to-do item exists, but this time utilizing aliases:

```
describe('Sharing Context between hooks and tests', () => {
    beforeEach(() => {
      cy.visit('http://todomvc.com/examples/react/#/');
```

```
        cy.get(".new-todo").type("New Todo {Enter}");
        cy.get('.todo-list>li:nth-
          child(1)').invoke('text').as('todoItem');
      });

      it('gets added todo item', function () {
        // todo item text is available for use
        expect(this.todoItem).to.eq('New Todo');
      });
    });
```

In the preceding code block, we can verify that Mocha has `this.todoItem` in its context and runs successfully, validating that the to-do item was indeed created. A further verification of the test can be done as shown in the following screenshot, which highlights the passing state of the Cypress test after the use of aliasing to reference the created to-do item in our to-do list:

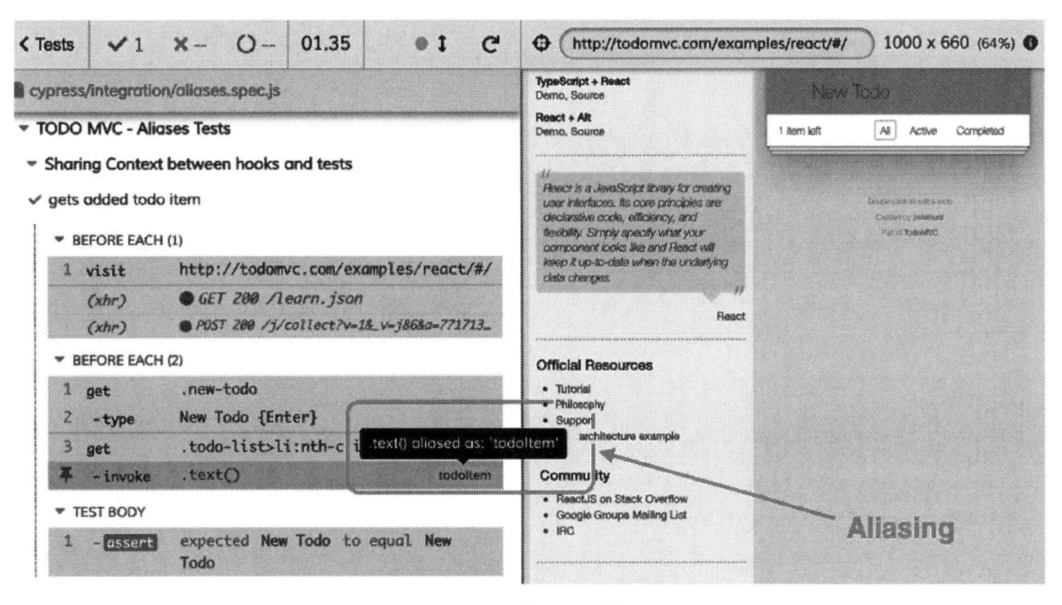

Figure 8.4 – Context sharing

In *Figure 8.4*, we see that Cypress highlights the aliased text and shows how it is invoked in our test. Cypress prints out the aliased elements and commands that have been used, making it easy to identify and debug in the event of a failure and to trace what caused that failure in the aliased elements.

> **Important note**
>
> It is not possible to use `this.*` with arrow functions in your Cypress tests as `this.*` will refer to the **lexical context** of the arrow function, and not that of Mocha's context. For any use of the `this` keyword, you will need to switch your Cypress tests to use regular `function () {}` syntax instead of `() => {}`.

Another great use of aliasing for sharing contexts is with Cypress fixtures. Fixtures are a feature that Cypress uses to provide mock data to be used in the tests. Fixtures are created in files and can be accessible in tests.

> **Important note**
>
> Fixtures provide test data, and we utilize fixtures to provide data that is consistent with either the input that the application would expect or the output that it would generate when an operation is carried out. Fixtures are an easy way for us to provide data inputs to our tests without going through the hurdles of hardcoding the data in our tests or auto generating the data when our tests are running. With fixtures, we can also utilize the same set of test data for different tests.

Assuming that we had a `todos fixture` that contained a list of all our created to-do items, we could have a test that is similar to the following code block:

```
describe('Todo fixtures', () => {
    beforeEach(() => {
      // alias the todos fixtures
      cy.get(".new-todo").type("New Todo {Enter}");
      cy.get('.todo-list>li:nth-
        child(1)').invoke('text').as('todoItem')
      cy.fixture('todos.json').as('todos')
    })

    it('todo fixtures have name', function () {
```

```
        // access the todos property
        const todos = this.todos[0]

        // make sure the first todo item contains the first
        // todo item name
        expect(this.todoItem).to.contain(todos.name)
      })
    })
```

In the preceding code block, we have aliased both the created to-do item and also the `todos.json` fixture file containing the created to-do items. We can utilize the to-do items' fixtures throughout all our tests, as we loaded the fixtures in the `beforeEach` hook of our tests. In this test, we accessed our first fixture value using `this.todo[0]`, which is the first object in our array of to-do items. To further understand how to work with fixtures and the exact files we are working with, take a look at the GitHub repository that we cloned at the beginning of this chapter, under `cypress/fixtures` directory.

> **Important note**
>
> Cypress still works using asynchronous commands, and trying to access the `this.todos` outside the `beforeEach` hook will lead to a test failure as the test first needs to load the fixtures before it can utilize them.

While sharing context, Cypress commands can also make use of a special `'@'` command, which eliminates the use of `this.*` when referring to the context of the declared aliases. The following code block shows the usage of `'@'` syntax when referring to Cypress aliases:

```
  it('todo fixtures have name', () => {
        // access the todos property
        cy.get('@todos').then((todos) => {
          const todo = todos[0]
        // make sure the first todo item contains the first
        // todo item name
        expect(this.todoItem).to.contain(todo.name)
        });
      });
```

In the preceding code block, we used the `cy.get()` command to eliminate the `this.*` syntax when accessing our fixture file, along with the need to use the old-style function declaration method. When we use `this.todos`, we are accessing the `todos` object synchronously, whereas when we introduce `cy.get('@todos')`, we are asynchronously accessing the `todos` object.

As mentioned earlier, when Cypress runs code synchronously, the commands are executed in the order in which they are called. On the other hand, when we run Cypress tests asynchronously, the responses from the executed commands are not returned in the order in which the commands were called, since the execution of the commands doesn't happen in the order in which they are called. In our case, `this.todo` will execute as a synchronous command, which will return `todo` object results in the order of execution, while `cy.get('@todos')` will behave like an asynchronous command and will return the `todo` object responses when they become available.

Accessing element references

Aliases can also be used to access DOM elements for reuse. Making references to elements ensures that we do not need to redeclare DOM elements once they have been referenced by an alias. In the following code block, we will create an alias for the input element for adding a new to-do item, and later reference it when creating our to-do items:

```
it('can add a todo - DOM element access reference', () => {
        cy.get(".new-todo").as('todoInput');
        // Aliased todo input element
        cy.get('@todoInput').type("New Todo {Enter}");
        cy.get('@todoInput').type("Another New Todo {Enter}");
        cy.get(".todo-list").find('li').should('have.length', 2)
  });
```

This test shows the use of aliases to access elements in the DOM that have been stored as references. In the test, Cypress looks for our saved `'todoInput'` reference and uses it instead of running another query to find our input item.

Accessing route references

We can use aliases to reference routes for an application under test. Routes manage the behavior of network requests, and by using aliases, we can ensure that proper requests are made, server requests are sent, and proper XHR object assertions are created when we make our requests. The following code block shows the usage of aliases when working with routes:

```
it('can wait for a todo response', () => {
      cy.server()
      cy.intercept('POST', '/todos', { id: 123
}).as('todoItem')
      cy.get('form').submit()
      cy.wait('@todoItem').its('requestBody')
        .should('have.property', 'name', 'New Todo')
      cy.contains('Successfully created item: New Todo')
    });
```

In this code block, we have referenced our `todoItem` request as an alias. The route request will then check whether the form that we submitted has been submitted successfully and returns a response. When using aliases in routes, we do not have to keep referencing or calling the route, as Cypress will already have a stored response of the route from the alias that we created earlier.

Accessing request references

Just like when accessing route references with aliases, we can use Cypress to access Cypress requests and use the properties of the requests later. In the following code block, we identify a request for a specific comment and check the properties of the comment using aliases:

```
it('can wait for a comment response', () => {
      cy.request('https://jsonplaceholder.cypress.io/
comments/6')
    .as('sixthComment');
      cy.get('@sixthComment').should((response) => {
        expect(response.body.id).to.eq(6)
    });
  });
```

The test makes an assertion on a specific comment and checks whether the assertion matches the ID of the comment. We have used an alias to reference the request URL in such a way that when running our tests, we just need to reference the URL that we have aliased without necessarily typing it in whole. The following screenshot of the running test shows how Cypress creates an alias that it later references while it is running the test:

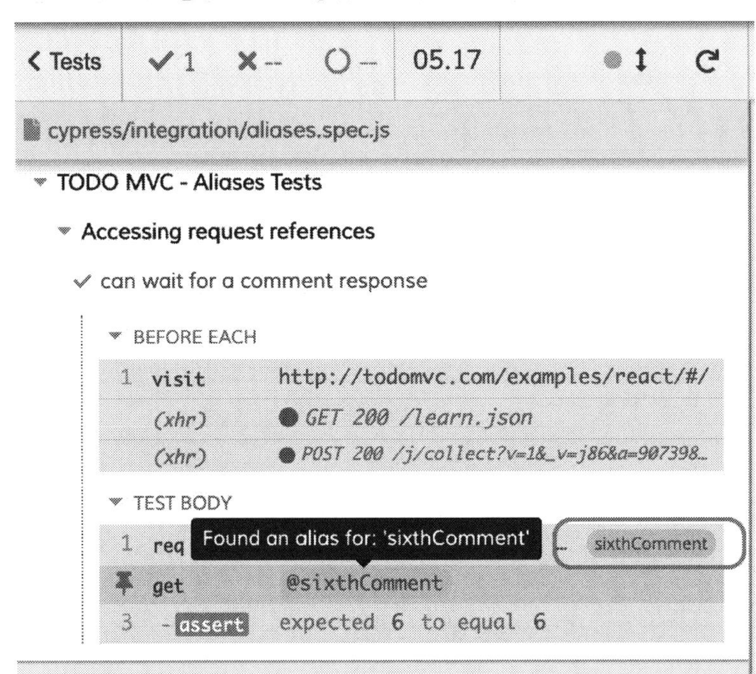

Figure 8.5 – Request references

In the preceding screenshot, the first `sixthComment` command is a command where Cypress is creating the alias, and the second is when the running test identifies the alias and asserts the expectation against the responses gotten from the aliased URL.

Recap – Understanding Cypress aliases

In this section, we learned about aliases and how they are used to write "clean" code for our tests by providing a way for us to access and have references to requests, elements, routes, and commands that we may later require in our tests. We have also learned how Cypress aliases are accessed: either through the asynchronous method that utilizes the @ symbol before the alias, or the synchronous method that directly accesses the aliased object using the `this` keyword. Finally, we learned how to utilize aliases in tests for referencing elements, enabling us to use aliased routes and requests in our tests.

Summary

In this chapter, we learned about aliases and variables and how to utilize them in Cypress. We covered what variables are in Cypress tests, different types of variables and their scopes, and how to utilize them. We also covered how variables in Cypress assist in the creation of closures and how we create an environment that can only be accessed by the variables in addition to the global context accessible to the tests. Lastly, we looked at how we use aliases and the different contexts in which aliases are utilized. We learned how to reference aliases in tests, how to use them with elements, routes, and requests, and even for context sharing between test hooks and the tests themselves.

From this chapter, you have gained the skills of understanding how aliases and variables work, how aliases can be used in both asynchronous and synchronous scenarios, and how and when to create and implement the scope of variables in tests.

Now that you fully understand how aliases and variables work, we are ready for our next chapter in which we will understand how the test runner works. We will dive into different aspects of the test runner and how to interpret events happening on the test runner.

9
Advanced Uses of Cypress Test Runner

Before we get started on advanced uses of the Test Runner, it is crucial that you understand how Cypress works, the role of the Test Runner, and how tests are executed in the Test Runner. This chapter builds on the knowledge of Cypress that you have acquired in the previous eight chapters and will focus on assisting you to understand the advanced functions of the Test Runner that we have not yet explored in this book.

Throughout this chapter, we will utilize the Test Runner and learn how to write better tests by making use of the built-in functions of the Test Runner. By learning how to use the Test Runner, we will have a deeper understanding of how tests run, what happens when they are failing, and how they can be improved. We will cover the following key topics in this chapter:

- Understanding the instrument panel
- Understanding the Selector Playground
- Test Runner keyboard shortcuts

Once you've worked through each of these topics, you will have a full understanding of the Test Runner and how to fully utilize it in the process of writing your tests.

Technical requirements

To get started, we recommend you clone the repository containing the source code and all the tests that we will write in this chapter from GitHub.

> **Important note**
>
> We have covered how to read and interpret Cypress errors in the Test Runner in *Chapter 5, Debugging Cypress Tests*. In that chapter, we also covered how we can interact with DOM snapshots in the Test Runner, where we covered the interaction between elements and the command log. In this chapter, we might make references to *Chapter 5, Debugging Cypress Tests*, or further expound on the information provided in that chapter.

The GitHub repository for this chapter can be found at `https://github.com/PacktPublishing/End-to-End-Web-Testing-with-Cypress`.

The source code for this chapter can be found in the `chapter-09` directory.

Understanding the instrument panel

The instrument panel is a special panel in the Cypress Test Runner that is only visible when Cypress is providing you with additional information about your tests. The appearance of the instrument panel is triggered by specific commands that provide more information about the tests. The commands that trigger the instrument panel include `cy.stub()`, `cy.intercept()`, and `cy.spy()`. In this section, we will explore how we can use the instrument panel to display additional information about tests.

To achieve our goal of understanding how the instrument panel works, we will have to understand how **intercepts**, **stubs**, and **spies** work, along with what specific information is displayed on the instrument panel when stubs, routes, and spies are called in Cypress tests.

Intercepts

Cypress uses the `cy.intercept()` command to manage the behavior of HTTP requests in the network layer of a test. To understand intercepts, we first need to understand how network requests take place in Cypress. Cypress automatically indicates on the Test Runner when an **XHR** (**XMLHttpRequest**) request is made from the running test. Cypress additionally creates a DOM snapshot of the moment when the request was called and when the response was received, which gives us an idea of what the DOM was like before and after the request. The following code block is an example of a request to get the response to an XHR request from our Todo application:

```
describe(Routing a request', () => {
    it('can wait for a app initialization, () => {
     cy.intercept('POST','**/j/**
      ').as('initializeTodoApp');
       cy.visit('http://todomvc.com/examples/react/#/');
       cy.wait('@initializeTodoApp'); // wait for intercept
       response
    })
  });
```

The preceding code block shows Cypress' `cy.intercept()` command listening for an XHR response that it expects Cypress to make on initialization of the application. In the test, we are verifying that the request was indeed made to the application, as we are waiting for the route response to have been called before our test completes execution.

Cypress has the capability to interpret requests, which makes it easy for the framework to manage HTTP requests by listening to the HTTP requests that the tests are making and knowing the responses that are returned by the request calls.

Intercepts in Cypress, using the `cy.intercept()` command, provide the ability to override XHR responses returned by the requests made by Cypress tests during execution. Overriding the XHR responses made by our application is what we call **stubbing** and we will look at this concept later in this chapter.

Cypress logs all the intercepts information on the instrument panel, and by looking at the panel, we can tell the number of matched routes in our tests, whether there were any responses that matched our routes, and whether they are stubbed or not. The following screenshot illustrates the use of the instrument panel to elaborate the information logged by Cypress concerning the routes:

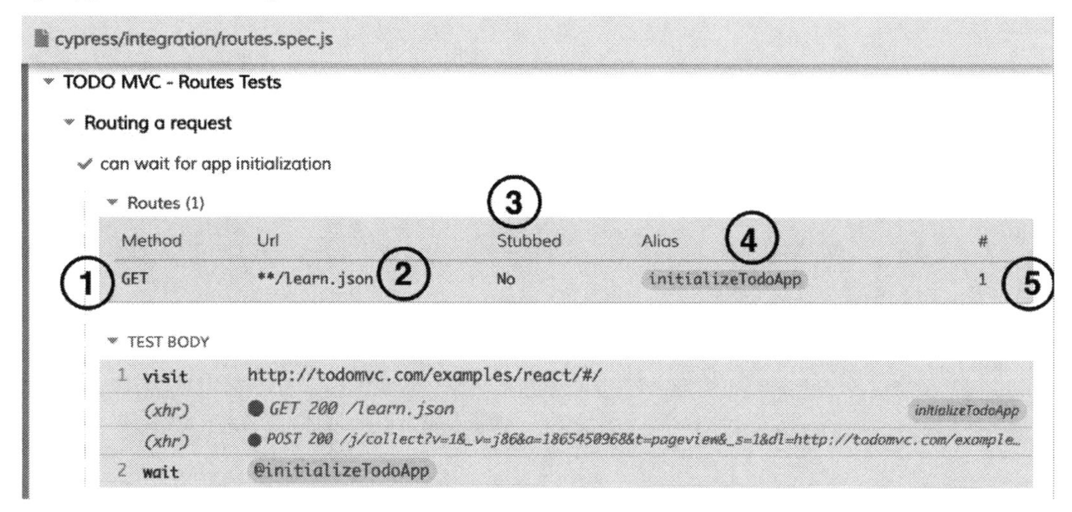

Figure 9.1 – Cypress instrument panel

Figure 9.1 shows the area represented by the instrument panel labeled **Routes** and in it, it contains columns of different types of information that the route responses have when a test has completed running. The different columns in the instrument panel for the routes have different purposes and are significant to both the running test and the instrument panel. The following are the different columns, each described with its use and significance in Cypress routing:

- **Method** (**1**): The **Method** column represents the request that the `cy.intercept()` command is expecting, and depending on the expected request, it can either be **GET**, **POST**, **PUT**, **PATCH**, or even **DELETE**.
- **Url** (**2**): The **Url** column will display the URL expected by our `cy.intercept()` command when running the Cypress tests. In this case, we have told Cypress to look for any route that ends with `learn.json` and if it encounters it then our test should pass.
- **Stubbed** (**3**): The **Stubbed** column will show whether our route has been stubbed or not. When a route is stubbed, Cypress will not return the response that was received, but the response that we pass to the route.

- **Alias (4)**: The **Alias** column shows the aliases that we have given our route in Cypress. In *Chapter 8, Understanding Variables and Aliases in Cypress*, we learned about aliases and how they can be useful when we need to access the information of an element, a route, or even a request. The alias provided in the **Alias** column is what we use to call our route, and this we will do by appending an @ prefix before the alias.
- **# (5)**: This match column will show the count of the responses that matched our route. In our case, the request to our URL was only made once and therefore our route was only called once in our tests.

The instrument panel information on the routes is sufficient for you to understand if any XHR requests were made to the routes that have already been declared in our tests and if the methods and number of request times are consistent with what is expected in the application.

Stubs

Stubs in Cypress are used to replace a function, control its behavior, or record its usage. Stubs can be used to replace actual methods with synthetic responses that we write ourselves. In the following code block, we will just verify that we can stub a method called `foo` when our test runs:

```
it('can stub a method', () => {
      let obj = {
        foo () {},
      }
      const stub = cy.stub(obj, 'foo').as('foo')
      obj.foo('foo', 'bar')
      expect(stub).to.be.called
    })
```

The `foo()` method shown in the preceding code block illustrates stubbing in action and from the code, we can see that we are expecting Cypress to know that our stub was called when the `foo` function is called from the test. The following screenshot shows the test executing and the details of the passed tests with the type of stub, stub name, and the number of times the stub was called:

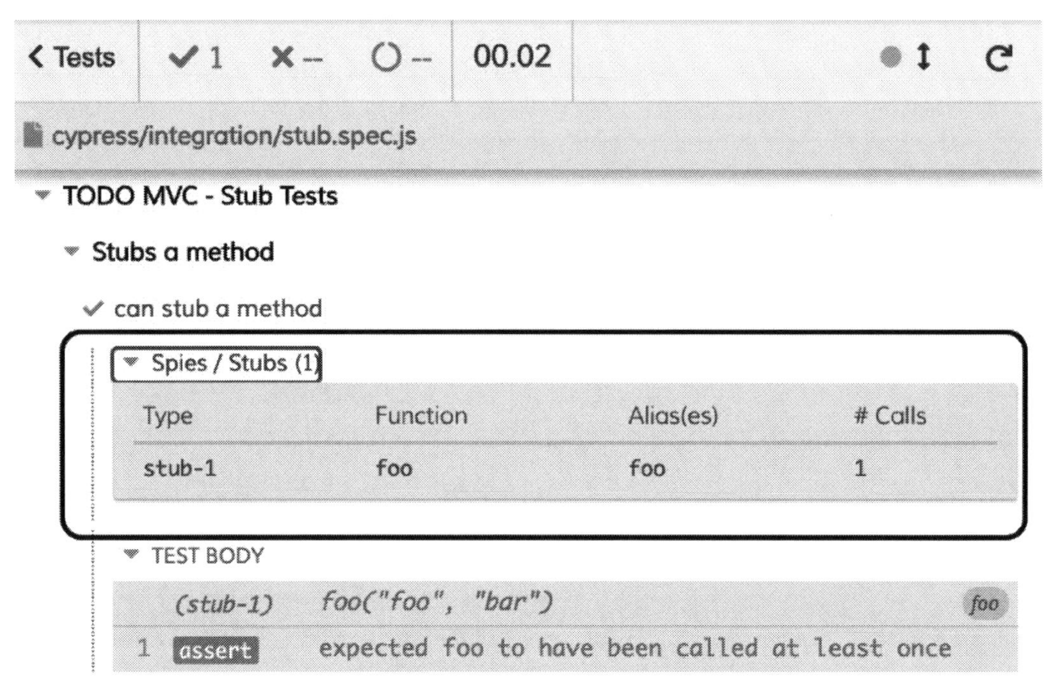

Figure 9.2 – Cypress stubbing

In *Figure 9.2*, Cypress shows our created stubs in the instrument panel and also shows the number of times the stubs were called during the execution of our tests. Stubbing comes in handy as we can stub out dependencies or functions that we do not necessarily want to test in our scope.

Spies

Spies behave just like stubs, with the difference that they wrap a method in the spy for them to record the calls and the arguments to the function. Spies are only used for verification of working elements or methods in Cypress. The most common use in tests is to verify that certain calls were made in the test and not necessarily for changing the expectations of the calls as in the case of stubs. The following screenshot shows the spy of a method where we verify that the `foo` method was called inside our `cy.spy()` method:

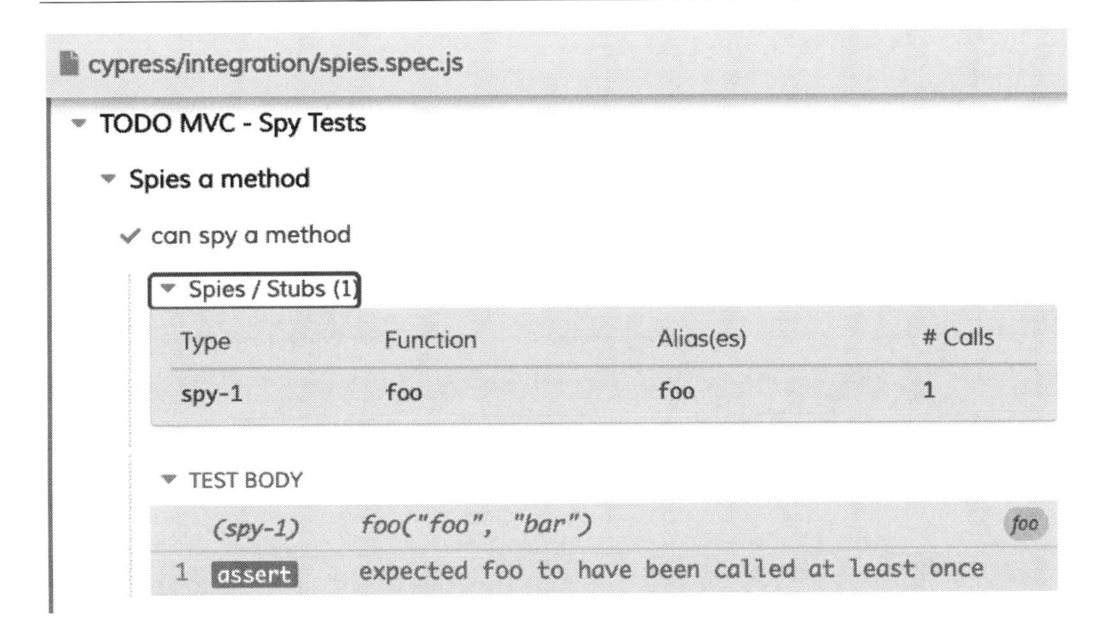

Figure 9.3 – Cypress spying

In *Figure 9.3*, the instrument panel plays a crucial role in showing us calls that were made to our `spy` function, what the name of the function is, the aliases allocated to our spy method, and the type of our test method.

Recap – understanding the instrument panel

In this section, we learned how we can utilize the instrument panel to understand intercepts, spies, and stubs in Cypress. We also learned how intercepts, spies, and stubs actually work and how the information on the instrument panel is useful to understand whether our implementation is correct. In the next section, we will dive into understanding the Selector Playground in Cypress and see how it works.

Understanding the Selector Playground

The Selector Playground is an interactive feature of the Cypress Test Runner. The Selector Playground gives you the ability to determine unique selectors, check elements that match a specific selector, and check the elements that match a specific text in the Cypress application. In this section, we will look at different strategies that Cypress uses to select elements and how from the Test Runner we can identify the selectors that we can use in our tests. By the end of this section, you will learn how to use Cypress to uniquely select elements using the Selector Playground and also how to use the selector strategies that Cypress utilizes to run tests.

Selecting unique elements

The Selector Playground could be one of the most underutilized features in the Cypress Test Runner, but also one of the most useful for anyone who wants to write tests that have meaningful selectors. The Selector Playground enables us to identify valid selectors and unique selectors for elements in our test application.

In the Selector Playground, Cypress calculates a unique selector for the targeted element and determines the selector by evaluating built-in selector strategies that are enabled by default in the test framework. The following shows two added todo items and an open Cypress Selector Playground showing how we can uniquely select any of the todo items:

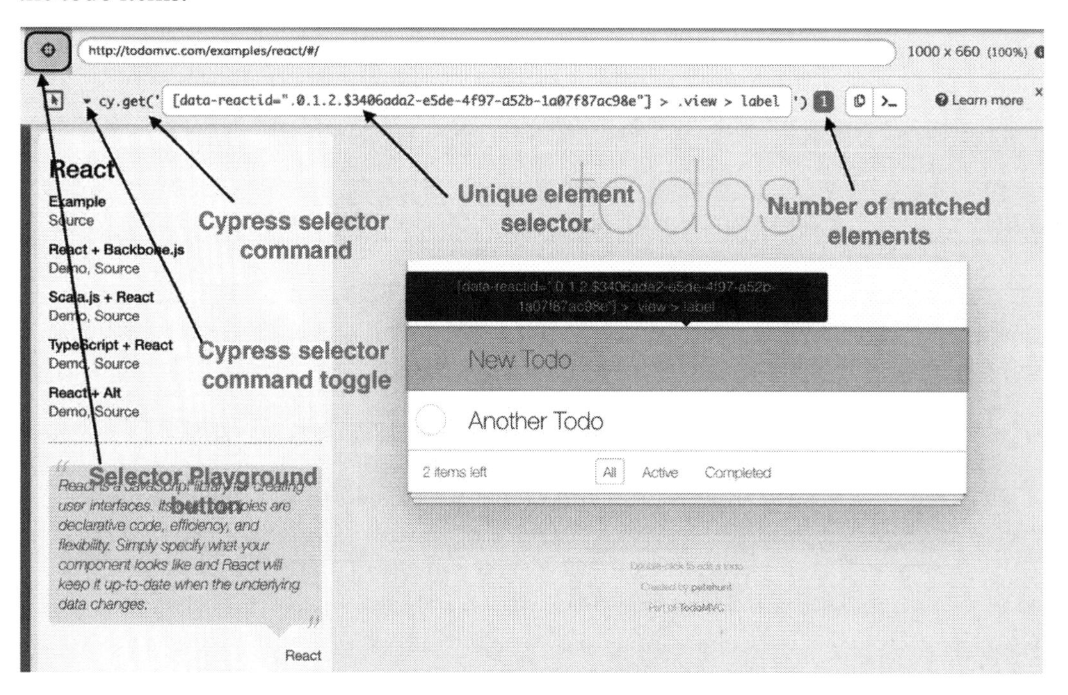

Figure 9.4 – Cypress Selector Playground

The first step is to click the Selector Playground button and once you click on it, the Selector Playground menu appears as shown in *Figure 9.4*. In the Selector Playground menu, you have the option to change the type of selector to either select elements with their selectors using `cy.get()` or using the element text, which can be found by toggling the selector to be `cy.contains()`. Inside, either the `cy.get()` command or the `cy.contains()` command is the specific element or text that we want to get from our application preview. For any element or text to qualify to be a unique element selector, the number of matched elements, represented by the gray color on the Selector Playground, should be **1** in order to ensure that we do not have duplicates of the element or the text. The buttons next to the label of the matched elements represent a copy command to copy the selector to the clipboard, while the next button is a print button that will print our selected or chosen command to the browser's console log.

When the mouse button below the Selector Playground is clicked, Cypress automatically shows a popup when a user hovers over an element and automatically selects a unique selector that can be used to identify the element in our tests. In *Figure 9.4*, we can see that once the **New Todo** item is hovered over, Cypress shows the unique selector as a tooltip and also populates the `cy.get()` command when the element is clicked. When an element is selected on the Selector Playground menu, Cypress will return the unique selector on the Selector Playground.

Determination of selectors

For Cypress to determine unique selectors in the Selector Playground, it uses a strategy of preference where the selectors selected are based on a series of strategies known to Cypress. Cypress has a preference for the following strategies when selecting and allocating unique selectors to elements:

- `data-cy`
- `data-test`
- `data-testid`
- `id`
- `class`
- `tag`
- `attributes`
- `nth-child`

> **Important note**
>
> The Selector Playground prefers selector strategies that begin with `data-*` in their identification format. In most instances, the selector strategies are custom and therefore eliminate the chances of flaky tests due to the use of dynamic IDs, class names in an application, or a change of CSS due to content changes. With custom `data-*` tags, the selector identifiers do not change and can be persisted throughout the life cycle of the application.

When an element can be identified by any of these selector strategies, Cypress will then display the unique selector of the element. While these strategies are what Cypress prefers, it is possible to alter the configuration and make Cypress recognize your selector strategy by adding it to the list of recognizable selector strategies.

Editing selector elements

The Selector Playground gives users the ability to edit the selectors for the selected elements. Having the ability to edit the selector elements is important as a more targeted selection and a more refined selector tag can be generated in a way that Cypress may not be able to by itself. Cypress automatically recognizes the changes made to the Selector Playground and will highlight the Selector Playground in blue when there is a match for the edited selector elements, or in red if there was no match for the edited selector identifier in the Selector Playground of the application preview. *Figure 9.5* and *Figure 9.6* show editing the Selector Playground with correct element selectors and also with an incorrect element selector:

Figure 9.5 – Valid element selector in the Playground

In *Figure 9.5*, editing the Selector Playground with an invalid element selector shows an error and highlights the Selector Playground in red to show us that no element was found using the selector element that we provided. *Figure 9.6*, on the other hand, shows editing the Selector Playground element selector is successful:

Figure 9.6 – Invalid element selector in the Playground

As observed in *Figure 9.6*, we are able to select both of our todo items with the selector that we edited in the Selector Playground. The blue color shows that Cypress found the elements that we are searching for, and did this by showing a count of the elements on the right side of the element selector input in the Selector Playground.

Recap – understanding the Selector Playground

In this section, we learned what the Selector Playground is and how important it is when using the Test Runner to run our tests. We learned how we can use the Selector Playground to select elements, modify elements, and even select and copy unique elements from the application preview of the Cypress Test Runner. We also learned how Cypress identifies elements and the selector strategies that are preferred when selecting elements. Finally, we learned how we can edit the locators in the Selector Playground and how we can identify whether our selectors are valid or not. In the next section, we will look at how the keyboard shortcuts work on the Test Runner.

Test Runner keyboard shortcuts

Keyboard shortcuts come in handy especially when we do not want to perform manual actions on the browser that involve a series of steps. In this section, we will learn how to use three keyboard shortcuts to control the Cypress Test Runner and to run our tests effectively. With the Test Runner, we will perform common actions more quickly than we would when explicitly triggering the actions with the browser actions.

The following are the mappings of different keyboard keys and their associated actions:

- *R* – Rerunning the tests of a spec file(s)
- *S* – Stopping the running tests
- *F* – Viewing all tests in the spec window

These keyboard keys will trigger different actions on the Test Runner depending on the key presses made by the user.

Recap – Test Runner keyboard shortcuts

In this section, we learned how Cypress keyboard shortcuts can be used to control the common actions of the Test Runner using three keys on the keyboard. We also learned that performing actions using the keyboard yields quicker actions than when triggering the same actions using the browser actions.

Summary

In this chapter, we learned about the instrument panel, Selector Playground, and keyboard shortcuts in the Cypress Test Runner. We explored how the instrument panel works with stubs, spies, and routes and explored how routes, stubs, and spies work, and what information is shown in the instrument panel. We also looked at how the Selector Playground is utilized in Cypress and how we can leverage it to identify elements for the application under test, and also to optimize the selectors that Cypress uses to uniquely select elements. Finally, we learned what Cypress keyboard shortcuts do and what keys are mapped to the actions that are available using the browser functionality.

Now that we know and understand how different elements in Cypress tie together, we can go further to test our knowledge on the topics we have learned through our exercises. In the next chapter, we will test our knowledge on navigation, network requests, and navigation configuration options for tests.

Section 3: Automated Testing for Your Web Application

In this part of the book, you will be exposed to exercises that will help you put into context the knowledge you gained in the first and second sections. This section comprises the best practices when it comes to testing, as well as covering the use of Cypress to test large-scale applications.

In this section, we will cover the following chapters:

- *Chapter 10, Exercise – Navigation and Network Requests*
- *Chapter 11, Exercise – Stubbing and Spying XHR Requests*
- *Chapter 12, Visual Testing in Cypress*

10 Exercise – Navigation and Network Requests

Before we get started on this chapter, it is important for you to understand that our focus in this third section of the book will be based on exercises and examples that will help you hone your testing skills and build knowledge that we may not have been able to cover in the previous chapters of this book. We will take a hands-on approach in this section with the goal being to work on as many examples and exercises as possible. Before we dive into this chapter, it is critical that you have gone through every chapter and are now looking to build upon the theoretical knowledge that you gained as we learned how Cypress can be used for testing.

In this chapter, we will focus on exercises and examples that cover the following topics:

- Implementing navigation requests
- Implementing network requests
- Advanced navigation request configuration

Once you've worked through each of these exercises, you will have the confidence to become a better tester and to get into more complex testing in areas of navigation and network requests.

Technical requirements

To get started, it is recommended that you clone the repository that contains source code and all the tests that we will write in this chapter from GitHub.

The GitHub repository for this chapter can be found at `https://github.com/PacktPublishing/End-to-End-Web-Testing-with-Cypress`.

The source code for this chapter can be found in the `chapter-10` directory.

Inside our GitHub repository, we have a finance test application that we will use for our different examples and exercises on Cypress navigation and Cypress requests as we go through this chapter.

> **Important note: running commands in Windows**
>
> NB: The default Windows Command Prompt and PowerShell do not correctly resolve the directory locations.
>
> Kindly follow the Windows commands listed further that work exclusively on Windows operating systems suffixed with the word `*windows`.

To make sure the test application is running on your machine, run the following commands from the root folder directory of the application on your terminal in your machine.

The `npm run cypress-init` command will install the dependencies that the application requires to run and the `npm run cypress-app` command, on the other hand, will just start the application. Optionally, you can reset the application state using the `npm run cypress-app-reset` command. Resetting the application removes any data that has been added that was not part of the application, taking the application state back to when you cloned the repository. We can further run the commands in our terminal just as they are shown here:

```
$ cd cypress/chapter-10;
$ npm install -g yarn or sudo npm install -g yarn

$ npm run cypress-init; (for Linux or Mac OS)
```

```
$ npm run cypress-init-windows; (for Windows OS)

// run this command if it's the first time running the
application
or
$ npm run cypress-app (for Linux or Mac OS)
$ npm run cypress-app-windows; (for Windows OS)

// run this command if you had already run the application
previously

Optionally
$ npm run cypress-app-reset; (for Linux or Mac OS)
$ npm run cypress-app-reset-windows; (for Windows OS)

// run this command to reset the application state after
running your tests
```

> **Important note**
>
> We have two main folders in our `chapter-10` directory, one folder contains the application that we will use for our examples and testing exercises while the second folder contains our Cypress tests for our test application. To properly run our tests, we have to run both our application and the Cypress tests, as the tests run on the live application that runs locally on our machines. It is important to also note that the application will require us to use port *3000* for the frontend application and port *3001* for the backend application.

Mastering the preceding commands will ensure that you will be able to run the application, reset the application state, and even install the dependencies for your application. Let's now get started with navigation requests.

Implementing navigation requests

Cypress navigation involves the behavior of navigating to the web pages of an application. In a lot of the tests that we have covered in this book, you might remember that before the tests, we have the `cy.visit()` command, which contains the URL of the page we are navigating to or that is being tested. The `cy.visit()` command is an example of a navigation command and assists us in making navigation requests in our Cypress frontend tests. In this section, we will cover different Cypress navigation commands by using examples and also exercises. By the end of this section, we will have a deeper understanding of Cypress navigation commands, which will help us build on the navigation knowledge that we already have from previous chapters of this book.

cy.visit()

We use `cy.visit()` in Cypress to navigate to a remote page of the application under test. By using this command, we can also pass in configuration information to the command and configure options such as the method, URL, timeout options, and even query parameters; we will dive into the configuration options of this command later in this chapter.

In our GitHub repository, in the `chapter-10/cypress-realworld-app` directory, we have an application that we will use for our examples and also for our exercises.

> **Important note**
>
> Our finance application located in the `chapter-10/cypress-realworld-app` directory records transactions. With the application, we can create transactions by either requesting or paying users for the transactions that already exist in the application. We can see notifications of transactions that have taken place and can also view the contacts and the log of the transactions that have taken place.
>
> The application utilizes a JSON database and therefore it is a tad slow when loading all the data into our application. In our tests, we have implemented a "safety switch" to prevent flaky tests by ensuring that in the `beforeEach` method, we wait for all the initial **XHR** (**XMLHttpRequest**) requests to load data before we begin our test execution requests. See more information on the `beforeEach` method in the following code block.

In our first example, in `navigation.spec.js`, as shown in the following code block, we will use the `cy.visit()` command to navigate to the notification page of the application:

```
describe('Navigation Tests', () => {
    beforeEach(() => {
     cy.loginUser();
     cy.server();
     cy.intercept('bankAccounts').as('bankAccounts');
           cy.intercept('transactions/public').
as('transactions')
     ;
           cy.intercept('notifications').as('notifications');

           cy.wait('@bankAccounts');
           cy.wait('@transactions');
           cy.wait('@notifications');
});
    afterEach(() => { cy.logoutUser()});

    it('Navigates to notifications page', () => {
        cy.visit('notifications', { timeout: 30000 });
        cy.url().should('contain', 'notifications');
    });
});
```

This code block illustrates the usage of the `cy.visit()` command where we visit a remote URL to the notifications route (`http://localhost:3000/notifications`), then verify that the remote URL we visited is what we expected. In our navigation command, we have also added the timeout option, which ensures that, before failing the navigation test, Cypress will wait for 30 seconds for the "page load" event before it fails the test.

The following screenshot shows our test being executed and Cypress waiting for all the data that has to be loaded from our JSON database by waiting on the XHR requests being received from the backend:

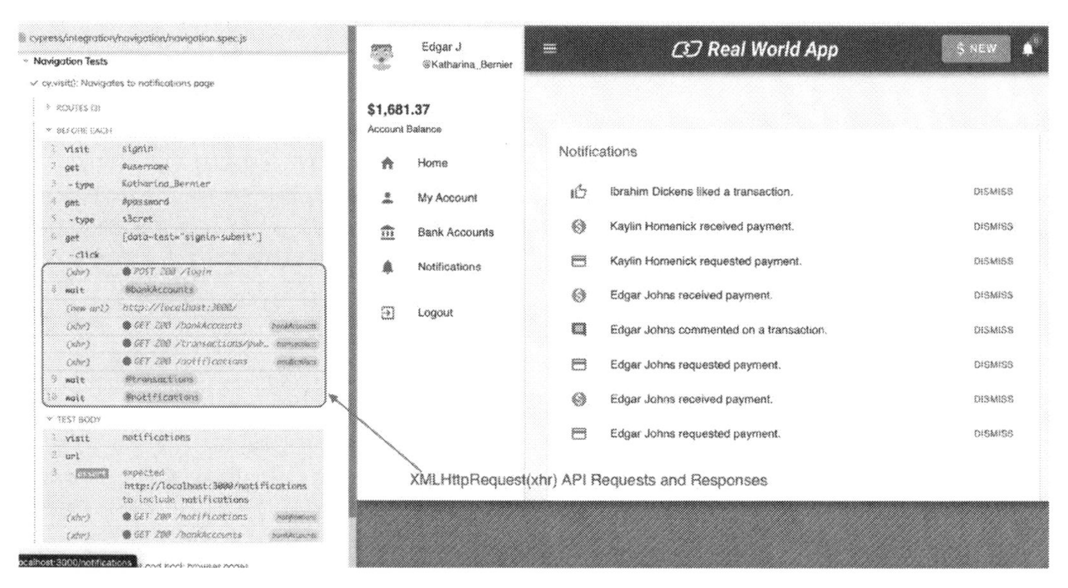

Figure 10.1 – XHR API requests and responses

In this screenshot, we are navigating to the `/signin` page, then after waiting for all the resources to be loaded, we are using the Cypress `cy.visit()` command to navigate to the `/notifications` page, which is visible on the right side on the test application preview. This is further validated by our test assertion, which validates that the visited URL contains the name `notifications`. The following exercise will help you better understand how to implement tests using the `cy.visit()` command.

Exercise 1

Using the financial application provided in the GitHub repository and located in the root directory in the `cypress-real-world-app` folder, carry out the following exercises to test your knowledge on the `cy.visit()` command:

1. Log in to our test application and navigate to the `http://localhost:3000/bankaccounts` URL using the `cy.visit()` command.
2. Create a new bank account, and then check whether or not the application redirects back to the `/bankaccounts` URL after the new bank account creation.

3. Log in to the application and, using the `cy.visit()` command, try to navigate to `http://localhost:3000/signin`.
4. After a successful login event for a test user, verify that the URL redirects to the dashboard instead of the `/signin` page.

The solutions to the exercise can be found in the `chapter-10/integration/navigation/navigation-exercise-solutions` directory.

This exercise will test your ability to understand the `cy.visit()` command, ensuring that, as a Cypress user, you can effectively use the command to navigate to different URLs and also pass in parameters and configuration options to the command.

cy.go()

The Cypress `cy.go()` navigation command enables a user to navigate forward or backward in the application under test. While using the `cy.go()` command, passing the `'back'` option to the command will lead the browser to navigate to the previous page of the browser history while the `'forward'` option will lead the browser to navigate to a forward history of the page. We can also use this command to click the forward and back button by passing in number options as parameters, where the `'-1'` option will navigate the application *back* while passing `'1'` will lead to *forward* navigation from the browser history.

By using `cy.go()`, we are able to manipulate the browser's navigation behavior by being able to step back to a previous page of a browser's history and also stepping forward to the next page of the browser's history.

> **Important note**
>
> We are only using `/bankaccounts` in our `cy.visit()` command as we have already declared `baseUrl` in our `cypress.json` file. `baseUrl` is the full version of the URL that we do not need to repeat every time we are using it in the `cy.visit()` and `cy.intercept()` commands. You can view more information in the GitHub repository that you cloned when starting this chapter.

In the following code block, we will use our finance application to verify that we can navigate back to the dashboard after navigating to the `/bankaccounts` page:

```
describe('Navigation Tests', () => {

    it('cy.go(): Navigates front and backward', () => {
```

```
        cy.visit('bankaccounts');
        cy.url().should('contain', '/bankaccounts');
        cy.go('back');
        cy.url().should('eq', 'http://localhost:3000/');
    });
});
```

In this test, after navigating to the /bankaccounts URL, we then use the Cypress inbuilt cy.go('back') command to navigate back to the dashboard URL, which we then verify that we have successfully navigated back to. The following exercise will shed more light on how to use the cy.go() command.

Exercise 2

Using the financial application provided in the GitHub repository and located in the chapter-10/cypress-real-world-app directory, carry out the following exercises to test your knowledge on the cy.go() command:

1. Once logged in, on the transactions dashboard, click on the **Friends** tab, and then on the **Mine** tab.
2. Use Cypress to navigate back to the **Friends** tab using the cy.go() command.
3. Once logged in, click on the **New** button located at the top right of the application navigation bar and create a new transaction.
4. Then navigate back to the dashboard page and back to the new transactions using the cy.go() Cypress command.

The solutions to the exercise can be found in the chapter-10/integration/navigation/navigation-exercise-solutions directory.

This exercise will help in building your skills for testing forward and back navigation using the cy.go() command. It will also assist in building your confidence when working with navigation when testing applications.

cy.reload()

The Cypress `cy.reload()` command is responsible for reloading a page. The command has only one set of options that can be passed to it, which is either to reload the page while clearing the cache or to reload the page with the cache being kept in the application memory. When a Boolean value of `true` is passed to the `cy.reload()` method, Cypress does not reload the page with the cache; instead, it clears the cache and loads new information about the page. The omission of the Boolean value leads Cypress to reload the page with the cache enabled. In the following code block, we are reloading the dashboard after logging into our application; this will refresh the state of our dashboard page:

```
it('cy.reload(): Navigates to notifications page', () => {
    cy.reload(true);
    });
```

In this test, if we had any cached items in our browser, Cypress will reload the page and invalidate the cache to ensure that a new state and cache of the page is created as our test is being executed. Let's look at the following exercise for more scenarios on the use of the `cy.reload()` command.

Exercise 3

Using the financial application provided in the GitHub repository and located in the `chapter-10/cypress-real-world-app` directory, carry out the following exercise to test your knowledge on the `cy.reload()` command:

1. Navigate to the **Account** menu item where we have the user settings.
2. Edit the first and second name of your test user, before clicking on the **Save** button.
3. Reload the page and verify that the `cy.reload()` command resets all the settings that were not yet saved.

The solutions to the exercise can be found in the `chapter-10/integration/navigation/navigation-exercise-solutions` directory.

In this exercise, we have learned that the reload command only resets items that are temporarily stored in the browser. By using the `cy.reload()` command, we have an understanding of how to reset the cached storage of our application and how to test it.

Recap – implementing navigation requests

In this section, we learned how navigation requests work on Cypress by evaluating examples and doing exercises. We also explored various navigation commands such as `cy.visit()`, `cy.go()`, and `cy.reload()`, which all play a major role when executing navigation requests in Cypress. In the next section, we will be looking at how we implement network requests using a hands-on approach of exercises and examples.

Implementing network requests

Network requests involve the handling of AJAX and XHR requests to the backend services. Cypress handles this with its in-built `cy.request()` and `cy.intercept()` commands. In this section, we will take a hands-on approach and dive deep into how we implement network requests in Cypress using examples and exercises. We have previously interacted with network requests in *Chapter 9, Advanced Uses of Cypress Test Runner*, of this book and this chapter will help you build on the theoretical knowledge and concepts that you are already familiar with.

cy.request()

The Cypress `cy.request()` command is responsible for making HTTP requests to API endpoints. This command can be used to execute API requests and receive responses without the need to create or import an external library to make and handle our API requests and responses. Our Cypress finance application uses a backend API that is based on a JSON database. To learn how the `cy.request()` command works, we will make requests to the database and check the responses. The following code block is a request to fetch all the transactions from our API:

```
it('cy.request(): fetch all transactions from our JSON
database', () => {
        cy.request({
            url: 'http://localhost:3001/transactions',
            method: 'GET',
        }).then((response) => {
            expect(response.status).to.eq(200);
            expect(response.body.results).to.be.an
            ('array');
        })
    });
```

In the preceding test, we are verifying that our backend responds with a `200` status code and with the transactions data, which is an array. We will learn more about the `cy.request()` command in the following exercise.

Exercise 4

Using the financial application provided in the GitHub repository and located in the `chapter-10/cypress-real-world-app` directory, carry out the following exercises to test your knowledge on the `cy.server()` command. The solutions to the exercise can be found in the `chapter-10/integration/navigation/network-requests-excercise-solutions` directory:

1. Once logged in, using your browser, investigate the XHR requests that are loaded by our `cypress-realworld` application when we first log in.
2. From the observation, write a test that returns data for the following:

   Contacts in the application

   Notifications in the application

By doing this exercise, you will have a better understanding of the `cy.request()` command and increase your knowledge of how Cypress requests work. Next, we will look at Cypress routing.

cy.intercept()

The `cy.intercept()` command manages the behavior of HTTP requests at the network layer of the tests. With the command, we can tell whether XHR requests were made and whether the responses to our requests match what we expect. We can even use the command to stub responses from routes. With `cy.intercept()`, we can dissect responses and ensure that we actually have the correct responses for our application under test. The `cy.intercept()` command gives us full access to all the HTTP requests of our Cypress tests at all stages.

> **Important note**
>
> We have to call `cy.intercept()` before we reference them in our tests so that the routes are recorded before we call them in our tests and, from the following test, we can observe that behavior in the `beforeEach()` command block. In the test that follows, we called the `cy.intercept` command before we started running our Cypress test.

In the following code block, found in the `network-request.spec.js` file, we are verifying that we have a response of the user information when a correct login request is made by the application under test:

```
describe('Netowork request routes', () => {
        beforeEach(() => {
        cy.intercept('POST','login').as('userInformation');
        });

        it('cy.intercept(): verify login XHR is called when
        user logs in', () => {
            cy.login();
            cy.wait('@userInformation').its('
            response.statusCode').should('eq', 200)
        });
    });
```

In this code block, we are verifying that the application made a `POST` request to the login endpoint and we received a successful status of `200`, which is a successful login. The `cy.login()` command navigates to the login page of the application. We will interact with the `cy.intercept()` command further in the following exercise.

Exercise 5

Using the financial application provided in the GitHub repository and located in the `chapter-10/cypress-real-world-app` directory, carry out the following exercises to test your knowledge on the `cy.intercept()` command. The solutions to the exercise can be found in the `chapter-10/integration/navigation/network-requests-exercise-solutions` directory:

1. Log in to the test application and navigate to the account page.
2. Use the Cypress `cy.route()` command to check whether Cypress verifies that a user is logged in when changing the user information.

Time for a quick recap.

Recap – implementing network requests

In this section, we explored how Cypress network requests work, and we did this by using examples and exercises to understand how `cy.request()` and `cy.intercept()` are utilized in Cypress tests. Using the examples and the exercises, we also got to expand our knowledge on how we use commands such as `cy.intercept()` to manipulate and stub. Now that we know about network requests and can comfortably write tests involving Cypress network requests, in the next section, we will dive into the advanced configuration of navigation requests.

Advanced navigation request configuration

Navigation is one of the most important aspects of properly running tests. By using the `cy.visit()`, `cy.go()`, and even `cy.reload()` commands, we have the ability to know what shortcuts to take when writing our tests. The navigation commands also significantly simplify test workflows. Most of the frontend tests require navigation and, therefore, grasping the advanced configuration will not only make your life easier but will also lead to a smoother experience while writing tests. In this section, we will focus mainly on the Cypress advanced command configuration for `cy.visit()` as it is the main navigation command for Cypress.

cy.visit() configuration options

The following table shows the configuration options for the `cy.visit()` command and the default values that are loaded when no options are passed to the option object:

Option	**Default**	**Description**
`url`	URL	URL
`retryOnNetworkFailure`	`true`	This option will retry the test when a network error is encountered when executing the test. The test will retry up to 4 times when this option is enabled.
`timeout`	Configured in the `cypress.json` file or the application default.	We can override the timeout option by increasing or decreasing the time it will take to resolve our visit our URL before throwing an error.

Option	Default	Description
`retryOnStatusCodeFailure`	`false`	The test will retry up to 4 times when this option is enabled and only when the test fails because of a status code error.
`auth`	null	This option will add the Basic Authorization headers to the `cy.visit()` request.
`qs`	null	Adding this will add query string parameters to the request.
`headers`	{}	This option will add headers to the `cy.visit()` request. It should be noted that Cypress only sends headers with the initial requests and not for the subsequent requests of the same type.
`method`	`GET`	Cypress only accepts a `GET` or a `POST` request for the `cy.visit()` command.

The `cy.visit()` command accepts different types of parameters and this determines the configuration and the options that are passed to it. The following are the parameters that the command accepts:

- Configuration with only the URL:

```
cy.visit(url)

e.g. cy.visit('https://test.com');
```

- Configuration with the URL and options as an object:

```
cy.visit(url, options)

e.g. cy.visit('https://test.com', {timeout: 20000});
```

- Configuration with only options as an object:

```
cy.visit(options);

e.g. cy.visit('{timeout: 30000}');
```

And it's recap time!

Recap – advanced navigation request configuration

In this section, we learned how we can configure the `cy.visit()` command using different options and also the different types of parameters that the command accepts. We also learned different default options that Cypress provides for us when they have none and have been passed with the `options` object, and this makes the process of using the `cy.visit()` command easy as we only provide to the command the options that we need to override in the test.

Summary

In this chapter, we learned how Cypress performs navigation, how requests are created, and how Cypress interprets and returns them for our test execution process. We took a hands-on approach to learning about the three fundamental Cypress navigation commands and also the three commands that Cypress uses for making and interpreting requests. The exercises provided a channel for you to get out of your comfort zone and do some research on advanced uses of Cypress and how we can integrate logic and the knowledge we have garnered in this book to write meaningful tests that add value to the applications being tested. Finally, we looked at the advanced configuration options of the `cy.visit()` command. I am confident that in this chapter, you learned the skills of handling and implementing navigation and network requests in tests and also configuring navigation requests.

Now that we have practically explored navigation and requests in Cypress using a hands-on approach, we will use the same approach in the next chapter to tackle stubbing and spying on tests using Cypress.

11 Exercise – Stubbing and Spying XHR Requests

Before we get started on this chapter, you need to understand why we need to stub or spy requests and methods, and to do this, you will need an understanding of Cypress requests and how to test individual methods. The previous chapters have presented extensive knowledge on how you can easily get started on Cypress, and we have covered concepts relating to network requests and functional testing. In this chapter, we will be building on the concepts that we have gained in the previous chapters with the focus being a hands-on approach by use of examples and exercises.

We will cover the following key topics in this chapter:

- Understanding XHR requests
- Understanding how to stub requests
- Understanding how to spy on methods in a test

Once you've worked through each of these topics, you will be ready to get started on visual testing with Cypress.

Technical requirements

To get started, we recommend that you clone the repository that contains the source code and all the tests, exercises, and solutions that we will write in this chapter from GitHub.

The GitHub repository for this chapter can be found at `https://github.com/PacktPublishing/End-to-End-Web-Testing-with-Cypress`. The source code for this chapter can be found in the `chapter-11` directory.

Inside our GitHub repository, we have a finance test application that we will use for the different examples and exercises of this chapter.

> **Important note: running commands in Windows**
>
> NB: The default Windows Command Prompt and PowerShell do not correctly resolve the directory locations.
>
> Kindly follow the Windows commands listed further that work exclusively on Windows operating systems suffixed with the word `*windows`.

To make sure the test application is running on your machine, run the following commands from the root folder directory of the application in the terminal on your machine:

```
$ cd cypress/chapter-11;
$ npm install -g yarn or sudo npm install -g yarn

$ npm run cypress-init; (for Linux or Mac OS)
$ npm run cypress-init-windows; (for Windows OS)

// run this command if it's the first time running the
application
or
$ npm run cypress-app (for Linux or Mac OS)
$ npm run cypress-app-windows; (for Windows OS)

// run this command if you had already run the application
previously

Optionally
$ npm run cypress-app-reset; (for Linux or Mac OS)
$ npm run cypress-app-reset-windows; (for Windows OS)
```

```
// run this command to reset the application state after
running your tests
```

> **Important note**
>
> We have our tests in the `chapter-11` directory and the test application located in the root directory of the repository. To properly run our tests, we have to run both our application and the Cypress tests, as the tests run on the live application that runs locally on our machines. It is important to also note that the application will require the use of port `3000` for the frontend application and port `3001` for the server application.

The first command will navigate to the `cypress-realworld-app` directory where our application is located. Then the `npm run cypress-init` command will install the dependencies that the application requires to run and the `npm run cypress-app` command will start the application. Optionally, you can reset the application state using the `npm run cypress-app-reset` command. Resetting the application removes any data that has been added that was not part of the application, taking the application state back to when you cloned the repository.

Understanding XHR requests

XMLHttpRequest (**XHR**) is an API that exists in all modern-day browsers and takes the form of an object whose methods are used to transfer data between a web browser sending the requests and the web server serving responses. The XHR API is unique as we can use it to update a browser page without reloading the page, request and receive server data after a page loads, and even send data to the server as a background task. In this section, we will cover the basics of XHR requests and their importance when it comes to the process of writing our Cypress tests.

Utilizing XHR requests in tests

XHR requests are a developer's dream as they allow you to *silently* send and receive data from the server without worrying about issues such as errors or waiting times when the client application needs to reload to perform an action. While XHR is a dream to developers, it is a nightmare for testers as it introduces uncertainties such as being unable to know when a request will finish processing and even when data has been returned from the server.

To solve the issue of XHR uncertainties, Cypress introduced the `cy.intercept()` command, which we have looked at in depth in both *Chapter 9, Advanced Uses of Cypress Test Runner,* and *Chapter 10, Exercise – Navigation and Network Requests,* in the network requests section. The `cy.intercept()` command listens to XHR responses and knows when Cypress has returned a response for a specific XHR request. With the `cy.intercept()` command, we can instruct Cypress to wait until the response for a particular request has been received, which makes it more deterministic when we are writing tests that wait for responses from a server.

The following code block from the `xhr-requests/xhr.spec.js` file shows the code to log a user into our finance test application. When a user is logged in, the application sends requests to the server to load the notifications, bank accounts, and transaction details that the application requires. These details are returned as XHR responses from the API server:

```
describe('XHR Requests', () => {

    it('logs in a user', () => {
        cy.intercept('bankAccounts').as('bankAccounts');
        cy.intercept('transactions/public').
        as('transactions');
        cy.intercept('notifications').as('notifications');

        cy.visit('signin');
        cy.get('#username').type('Katharina_Bernier');
        cy.get('#password').type('s3cret');
        cy.get('[data-test="signin-submit"]').click()

        cy.wait('@bankAccounts').its('response.statusCode'
        ).should('eq', 200);
        cy.wait('@transactions').its('response.statusCode
        ').should('eq', 304);
        cy.wait('@notifications').its('response.statusCode
        ').should('eq', 304);
    });
});
```

In the preceding code block, we are logging a user in and waiting for Cypress to return XHR responses to our transaction, notification, and bank account requests that are sent from the server. The responses are only sent when there is a successful user login attempt. We can visualize how Cypress handles XHR requests in a test in the following screenshot:

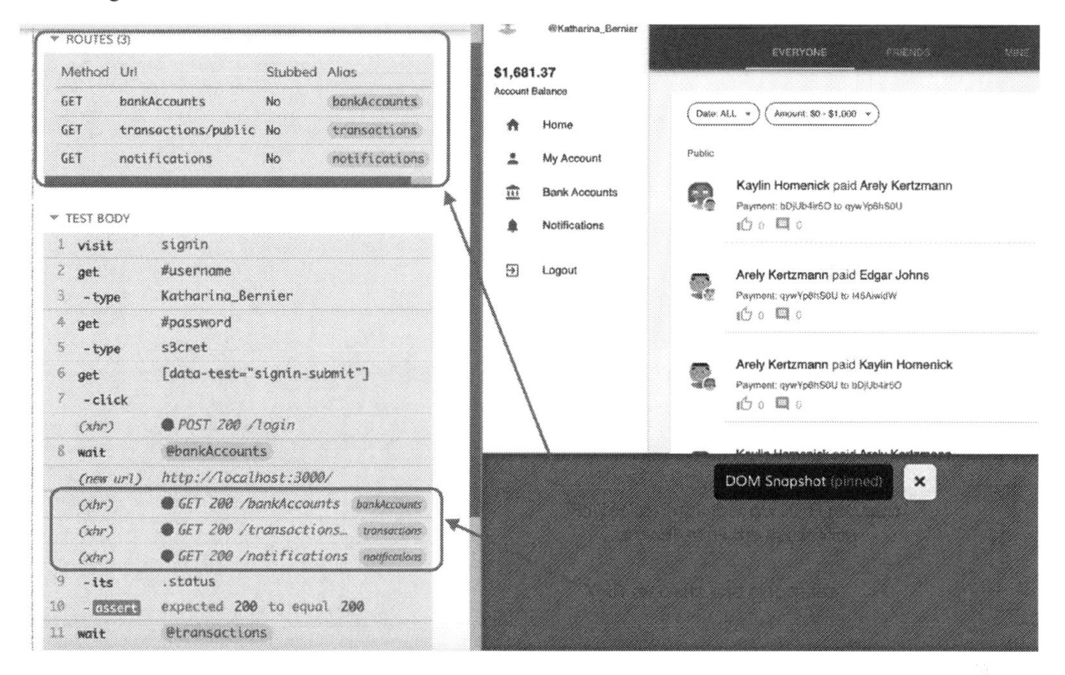

Figure 11.1 – XHR requests and responses from the server

This screenshot shows the application making XHR requests to our server for `/bankAccounts`, `/transactions`, and `/notifications`. For our test to be deterministic and for us to wait for a specified time to ensure a successful login, we use the `cy.intercept()` command to check when the responses from the XHR requests have been sent back by the server and whether they have been sent back with the correct status codes.

Waiting for XHR responses in tests gives us significant advantages over tests that do not have any *fail mechanisms* that handle waits or tests that have explicit time waits. The alternative to waiting for XHR responses is to explicitly wait for a specific amount of time, which is only an estimation and not the exact time that Cypress waits for a particular response. Some of the advantages of waiting for responses to routes while running our tests are as follows:

- Being able to assert the returned XHR response object from the route
- Creating tests that are robust, hence reducing flakiness

- Having failure messages that can be understood due to their preciseness
- Being able to stub responses and "fake" server responses

With these advantages highlighted, usage of XHR requests assists us to deterministically know when the responses are received and when Cypress can continue executing our commands, having received all the required responses for the application.

Recap – utilizing XHR requests in tests

In this section, we learned about XHR requests, what they are, and how Cypress utilizes them to send and fetch requests from the application server. We also learned how we can wait for XHR responses to reduce flaky tests by deterministically waiting for the responses from our server responses. We also learned how XHR can assist us, how we can have precise failure messages, and even how we can assert responses from our server responses. Finally, we went through how we can use the `cy.intercept()` command with XHR responses and the potential benefits of being able to control the execution of our tests by reducing test uncertainties. In the next section, we will look at using stubbing to control the XHR responses from the server.

Understanding how to stub requests

Now that we know what XHR requests are, it is important to know how we can help Cypress test XHR requests, and better still, how we can avoid actual responses from the server and instead create our own "fake" responses that our application will interpret as the actual responses that have been sent from the server. In this section, we will look at how we can stub XHR requests to the server, when to stub requests, and the impact of stubbing server requests in our tests.

Stubbing XHR requests

Cypress gives the flexibility of allowing users to either have their requests reach the server, or instead have stubbed responses when the requests to the server endpoints are made by the application. With the flexibility of Cypress, we even have the ability to allow some requests to pass through to the server while denying other requests and stubbing them instead. Stubbing XHR responses adds a layer of control to our tests. With stubbing, we are in control of the data returned to the client and we have access to change the response of the **body**, **status**, and **headers**, or even introduce a delay if we want to simulate network latency in the server response.

Advantages of stubbing requests

Having stubbed requests gives us more control over the responses that are returned to the tests and also over the data that will be received by the client making the requests to the server. The following are the advantages of stubbing our requests:

- Having control over the body, headers, and status of the responses.
- Quick response times of the responses.
- No required code changes to the server.
- Network delay simulations can be added to the request.

Next, let's also look at some disadvantages.

Disadvantages of stubbing requests

While stubbing is a good way of handling XHR responses to Cypress client applications under test, it also comes with some downsides to our testing process as highlighted here:

- The inability to have test coverage on some server endpoints
- No guarantee that the response data and stubbed data are a match

It is recommended to stub XHR responses in the majority of tests to reduce the amount of time it takes to execute tests and also to have a healthy mix of stubbed and actual API responses from the server. XHR stubbing in Cypress is also best suited when working with JSON APIs.

In the following code block, in the `xhr-requests/xhr-stubbing.spec.js` file, we are going to stub the `bankAccounts` endpoint and avoid making the actual requests to the server when we are running our application:

```
describe('XHR Stubbed Requests', () => {
    it('Stubs bank Account XHR server response', () => {
        cy.intercept('GET', 'bankAccounts',
        {results: [{id :"RskoB7r4Bic", userId :"t45AiwidW",
        bankName: "Test Bank Account", accountNumber
        :"6123387981", routingNumber :"851823229",
        isDeleted: false}]})
        .as('bankAccounts');
        cy.intercept('GET', 'transactions/public').
        as('transactions');
        cy.intercept('notifications').as('notifications');
```

```
            cy.wait('@transactions').its('
            response.statusCode').should('eq', 304);
            cy.wait('@notifications').its('
            response.statusCode').should('eq', 304);
            cy.wait('@bankAccounts').then((xhr) => {
                expect(xhr.response.body.results[0].
                bankName).to.eq('Test Bank Account')
                expect(xhr.response.body.results[0].
                accountNumber).to.eq('6123387981')
            });
        });
});
```

In the preceding code block, we have stubbed the `/bankaccounts` server response and instead of waiting for a response, we provided a response ourselves that is almost identical to the response that the server would have sent back. The following screenshot shows the successful stubbed response and the "fake" stubbed bank account information that we provided to our client using the stubbed response:

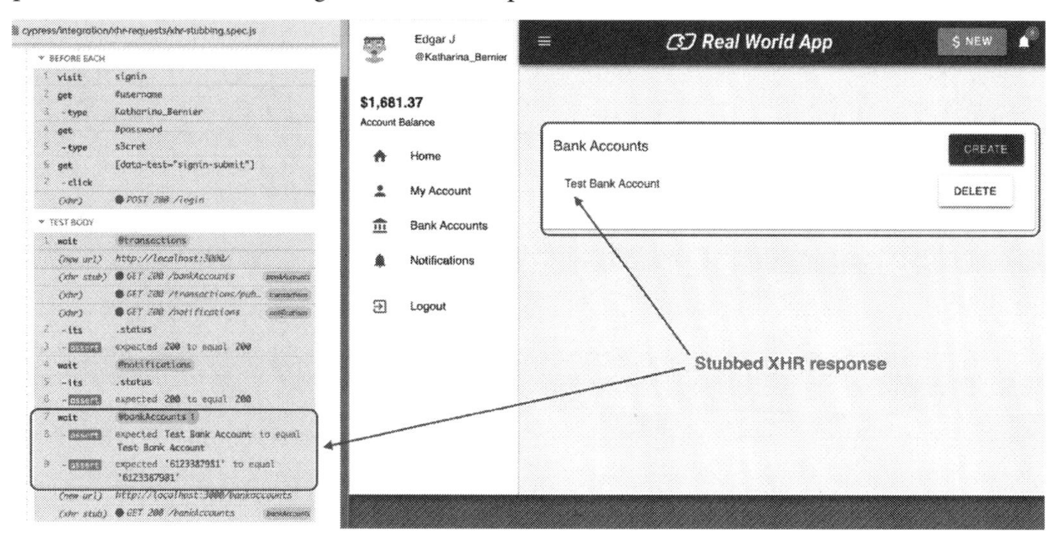

Figure 11.2 – Stubbed XHR response in the client application

In *Figure 11.2*, we can see that it is almost impossible to tell whether our response was stubbed or we received it from our server. With Cypress, it is impossible for the client application to recognize whether a response was genuinely sent from the server or was stubbed, a quality that makes Cypress an effective tool for intercepting requests and sending responses that would otherwise have taken a long time to be sent from the server. We will learn more about stubbing XHR responses in the following exercise.

Exercise 1

Using the financial application provided in the GitHub repository and located in the `cypress-realworld-app` directory, carry out the following exercise to test your knowledge on stubbing XHR responses. The solutions to the exercise can be found in the `chapter-11/integration/xhr-requests-exercises` directory:

1. Stub the login POST request of the application and instead of returning the name of the test user in the dashboard, change it to reflect your name and your username.

   Assert that the response returned does indeed have your username and name information that was stubbed. The following screenshot shows the information on the page that should change:

Figure 11.3 – Change the name and username by stubbing the login response

> **Important note**
>
> To properly stub a response, you need to understand what the server sends as a response when the route is not stubbed. To do this, open the browser console on your browser, click the **Network** tab, and then select the **XHR filter** option. You can now see all the responses and requests sent to the server and received by your client. To get the specific request to a stub, you should click the exact request and copy the response from the **Response** tab of the browser console's **Network** window. The exact response (or a response that is similar in structure) is what we should use to stub our server responses so as to ensure the consistency of responses to our client. From the **Network** window, we can also obtain information such as the headers sent and received with the request, and the actual URL that is used to send the requests to the server.

The following screenshot shows an example of the **notifications** XHR response from the server:

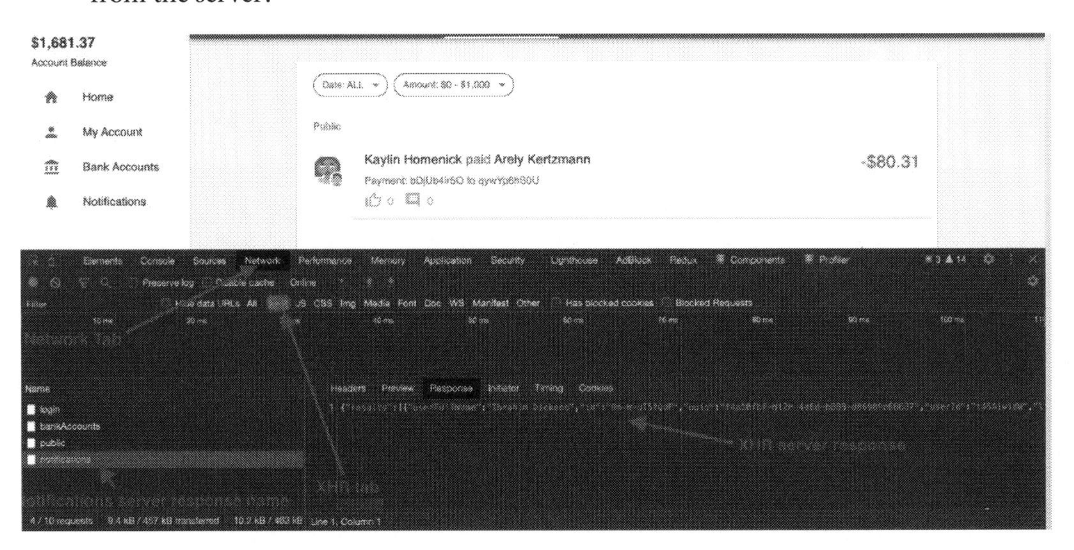

Figure 11.4 – Server XHR response for notifications endpoint on the Chrome browser console

2. After a successful login, select a random transaction from the `Everyone Dashboard` tab and modify the transaction amount to be $100.

From this exercise, you not only learned how to stub XHR responses but also how the client handles the data that it has received from the server. By understanding the benefits of XHR response stubbing, you are now ready to tackle complex Cypress tests that involve stubbed responses.

Recap – understanding how to stub requests

In this section, we learned how to use XHR server requests to receive requests and also to intercept the requests sent by using stubs. We also learned how with stubs, we can control the nature of the responses we send back to the client application, and also how we can assert our stubbed responses that look similar to the client responses that we receive from the server. Finally, we learned how we can use our browser to identify which responses to stub, and use the content of the responses that we are stubbing. In the next section, we will look at how spying works and how we can utilize it in our Cypress methods.

Understanding how to spy on methods in a test

Spies and stubs are closely related with the difference being that, unlike stubs, which can be used to modify data of a method or a request, spies only obtain the state of the method or request and do not have the ability to modify the method or the request. They work just like real-life spies who only track and report. Spies help us understand the execution of tests, what elements have been called, and what has been executed. In this section, we will learn about the concept of spying in Cypress, the advantages of spying on methods, and how we can utilize spying to write better Cypress tests.

Why spy?

We use spies in Cypress to record calls in a method along with the arguments of the method. By using spies, we can assert that a specific method was called a certain number of times and was called with the right arguments. We can even tell what the return values of a method were, or the execution context of the method at the time it was called. Spies are mostly used in the unit testing context but also have applications in the integration context, such as testing that two functions have proper integration with each other and that they work harmoniously when executed together. When executed, the `cy.spy()` command returns a value instead of a promise like almost all the other Cypress commands. The `cy.spy()` command does not have a timeout and cannot be chained further with other Cypress commands.

Advantages of spies

The following are some of the advantages of using spies in tests:

- Spies do not modify the requests or methods called.
- Spies give you the ability to quickly verify whether methods have been called.
- They offer an easy way to test functional integration.

Spying is an interesting concept as it introduces a way to monitor methods without necessarily taking an action on the outcome. In the following code block, we have a test that consists of a simple function to sum two numbers:

```
it('cy.spy(): calls sum method with arguments', () => {
        const obj = {
            sum(a, b) {
                return a + b
            }
        }
        const spyRequest = cy.spy(obj, 'sum').as('sumSpy');
        const spyRequestWithArgs = spyRequest.withArgs(1,
        2).as('sumSpyWithArgs')
        obj.sum(1, 2); //spy trigger
        expect(spyRequest).to.be.called;
        expect(spyRequestWithArgs).to.be.called;
        expect(spyRequest.returnValues[0]).to.eq(3);
    });
```

In the preceding method, we have set `cy.spy()` to monitor our `sum` method and trigger the spy when the method is called or when it is called with arguments. Whenever the method is called, our spy will record the number of times it was called, and we can also go ahead and check whether or not our method was called with any arguments. The `sum` function is inside a JavaScript object, and the trigger for the spy method is the `obj.sum(1, 2)` sum function call, which is called before our assertions are executed in the test. The following screenshot shows the spies, the number of calls, and the aliases of the test:

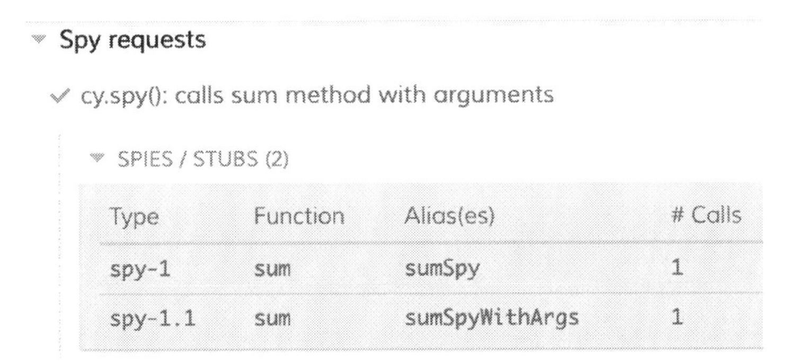

Figure 11.5 – Spying on a sum method

Looking at this method that uses the `cy.spy()` method on the `sum()` function, we can see that both the spies of the `sum` method and the `sum` method called with arguments were triggered once the `sum` method started executing.

In the next example, we will explore a more complex scenario where we will try to spy on a method that returns all the transactions in our JSON database from the server. The following code block shows the spy of the method that will fetch all of our transactions:

```
it('cy.spy(): fetches all transactions from our JSON database',
() => {
        const obj = {
          fetch(url, method) {
                return cy.request({
                    url,
                    method
                }).then((response) => response);
            }
        }

        const spyRequest = cy.spy(obj,
        'fetch').as('reqSpy');
        obj.fetch('http://localhost:3001/transactions',
        'GET');
        expect(spyRequest).to.be.called;
        expect(spyRequest.args[0][0]).to.eq
        ('http://localhost:3001/transactions')
        expect(spyRequest.args[0][1]).to.eq('GET');
    });
```

In this test, we are verifying that the request to fetch the transactions from the database takes place. With this test, we can monitor our method and check that the proper arguments are passed to our method when it is called.

It is clear that, with spies, we are able to identify which methods were called, how many times they were called, and what arguments were used when the method was called. We will learn more about spies in the following exercise.

Exercise 2

Using the financial application provided in the GitHub repository and located in the `cypress-realworld-app` directory, carry out the following exercises to test your knowledge of stubbing XHR responses. The solutions to the exercise can be found in the `chapter-11/integration/spies-exercise` directory:

1. Create a method called `Area` that calculates the area of a triangle, spy on the `area` method, and call the method to assert that indeed the `area` method is called and spied by `cy.spy()`. Assert that the method was also called with the `base` and `height` arguments.
2. Using our application, log in as a user and spy on the API request method to fetch all the bank accounts of that logged-in user. Assert that the method to make the API request to the server was called and that the arguments were passed as parameters to the method.

This exercise will assist you in understanding how spies work in Cypress and the different methods that can be used with `cy.spy()` to find the contents of the methods that are being spied on. By spying on methods, we are also able to tell whether or not the method arguments are called and how they were called, together with the return values.

Recap – understanding how to spy on methods in a test

In this section, we learned about spying, covering how important spying is and how different it is from stubbing, as we are not allowed to change the values of the method or the request being spied on. We also learned how we can use stubbing to identify the arguments of a method, the number of times a method was called, the execution context, and also the return values of the methods being spied on. Using the examples and the exercise, we also got to interact with the `cy.spy()` command, which helped us to understand the command and how it works in the context of methods.

Summary

This chapter's focus was mainly on XHR requests and responses and how they interact with the client and the server. We started by first understanding what XHR requests and responses are and how important they are when we want to send requests from the client and also receive requests from the server. In this chapter, we also looked at how we can "fake" server responses by stubbing XHR responses using the Cypress stub functionality that is built into the `cy.intercept()` command. Finally, we explored the Cypress `cy.spy()` command, which further gave us an idea of how we can monitor methods in Cypress and get the ability to find out the number of times the methods were executed, how they were executed, their arguments, and even their return values. In the final section, we learned the importance of knowing that with spying, we can only "observe" how the execution takes place, and not necessarily have the ability to change the execution process of the request or the methods that are being tested.

I believe that through this chapter, you have gained the skills of knowing what XHR requests are, how they work, how to stub them, and how to spy on Cypress methods. In the next chapter, we will look at visual testing in Cypress.

12
Visual Testing in Cypress

Before we get started with visual testing, you should have an idea of the other forms of testing and how we can use Cypress to accomplish this. The previous chapters of this book covered, at a basic to intermediate level, how to easily get started with Cypress, how to configure Cypress, and how you can optimize your use of Cypress to develop a more creative workflow for your test writing process. The background information in the previous chapters will provide you with the context required to tackle this chapter. Our focus in this last chapter of this book will be on visual testing using Cypress.

In this chapter, we will cover the basics of visual testing and understand why we need it. We will also learn about some of the tools we can use to carry out visual testing. The topics in this chapter will help you, as an engineer or a tester, understand why visual testing is important for web applications and how we can leverage it to write better tests.

We will cover the following key topics in this chapter:

- Visual testing
- Understanding viewports
- Visual testing tools in Cypress tests

Once you've worked through each of these topics, you will be ready to start your journey into the automation testing world with Cypress as your tool of choice.

Technical requirements

To get started, we recommend that you clone the GitHub repository for this book, which contains the source code and all the tests, exercises, and solutions that we will be writing in this chapter.

The GitHub repository for this chapter can be found at `https://github.com/PacktPublishing/End-to-End-Web-Testing-with-Cypress`.

The source code for this chapter can be found in the `chapter-12` directory.

Inside our GitHub repository, we have a finance test application that we will use for the different examples and exercises in this chapter.

> **Important note: Running commands in Windows**
>
> NB: The default Windows Command Prompt and PowerShell do not correctly resolve the directory locations.
>
> Kindly follow the Windows commands listed further that work exclusively on Windows operating systems suffixed with the word `*windows`.

To make sure the test application is running on your machine, run the following commands from the root folder directory of the repository on your machine's terminal:

```
$ cd cypress/chapter-12;
$ npm install -g yarn or sudo npm install -g yarn

$ npm run cypress-init; (for Linux or Mac OS)
$ npm run cypress-init-windows; (for Windows OS)

// run this command if it's the first time running the
application
or
$ npm run cypress-app (for Linux or Mac OS)
$ npm run cypress-app-windows; (for Windows OS)

// run this command if you had already run the application
previously

Optionally
$ npm run cypress-app-reset; (for Linux or Mac OS)
```

```
$ npm run cypress-app-reset-windows; (for Windows OS)
// run this command to reset the application state after
running your tests
```

> **Important note**
>
> We have our tests in the `chapter-12` directory and the test application located in the root directory of the repository. To run our tests properly, we have to run both our application and the Cypress tests since the tests run on the live application, which has to run locally on our machines. It is important to note that the test application will require the use of port `3000` for the frontend application and port `3001` for the server application.

The first command will navigate us to the `cypress-realworld-app` directory, which is where our application is located. The `npm run cypress-init` command will install the dependencies that the application requires to run, while the `npm run cypress-app` command will start the application. Optionally, you can reset the application state using the `npm run cypress-app-reset` command. Resetting the application removes any data that was added that was not part of the application, thus taking the application's state back to when you cloned the repository.

Visual testing

Whether you are a web developer or a tester, there is a need to ensure that the application under development retains the look and feel that was intended at project conception. As a developer, you may want to verify that there are no visual aspects about your application that changed between releases. As a tester, you may want to validate that the application's user interface remains consistent between releases and is consistent with the design.

Functional testing can be used to check for visual aspects, such as validating that a button or an input box is present. However, this may involve a lot of code being written and, most of the time, will not allow you to test every aspect of the application, such as CSS changes when we use it to validate user interface elements. Visual testing is the ability to verify visual aspects of an application's user interface and ensure that they are consistent with the expectations.

In this section, we will learn what visual testing is, what the different types of visual testing are, the differences between manual and automated visual testing, and when to use different types of visual testing approaches.

Why visual testing?

Visual testing takes a practical approach as you must directly map the visual aspects of a page and compare those aspects to the expected designs. It is possible to dismiss the idea of visual testing because we think that our eyes are accurate enough for validation purposes, which is a flawed assumption. While the naked eye can notice visible page changes, it is a little bit more difficult for the eye to detect minute details, such as a change in the CSS properties that made an input element move by several pixels or minimal pixel changes.

Visual testing exists to give both developers and testers confidence that a web page's user interface was not broken by any developer changes that were made. For instance, with visual testing, there is no need to fear if a version of the application that was deployed to the production environment is missing a signup button while previous versions of the application had it.

There are two types of visual testing, as follows:

- Manual visual testing
- Automated visual testing

These two types of visual testing will open our worlds up to how important visual testing is, as well as how we can take advantage of these two testing methods to write better tests.

Manual visual testing

Manual visual testing involves using the naked eye to validate whether the changes that were made by the development team did not break any visible user interface functionality. Manual visual testing involves either the testers or the development team visually testing the developed user interface and comparing it to the designs that were initially created. The process of visually testing the application confirms that there are no changes in the behavior, look, and feel of the user interface that were not intended. Manual visual testing is good and suitable for small changes in the user interface, but this may not be a very accurate way of validating an application with a lot of pages and visual elements or different viewports. To identify the limitations of manual visual testing, the following image, by *Atlantide Phototravel*, shows a side-by-side comparison of the Eiffel tower. They are very similar but minute details have been omitted in the second frame. Take a few seconds to compare the images and try to find the visual differences without looking at the rounded regions in the second image:

Figure 12.1 – Spotting the differences in the Eiffel Tower image

Even to the trained eye, there are details such as bird patterns, missing people, and even missing clouds that could make it almost visually impossible to tell if there is actually a difference between the two photographs. By applying the same idea of manual visual testing, it is very possible to miss details and not be able to find any differences between them, even when some elements are missing or have been added to the applications under test.

Automated visual testing

Automated visual testing involves testing the visual elements of the page. Instead of using a manual approach, an automated process to check the consistency of the application pages is used. To run automated visual tests properly, we must save and define our desired user interface as a **baseline**. We can then use this in our tests to check whether we need to update the baseline or modify the changes made to our application.

Automated visual testing has its roots in functional testing. Instead of asserting every element in a page and also checking the properties of the elements in a page, automated visual testing takes the approach of checking the entire page with a single assertion.

There are two types of automated visual testing:

- Snapshot testing
- Visual AI testing

Let's look at each of them in detail.

Snapshot testing

Snapshot testing is a type of automated visual testing where a raster graphic or a bitmap of a specific screen is recorded when the test is running. The recorded bitmap is then checked against the baseline bitmap that was recorded previously (baseline). The algorithms in the snapshot testing tools only check whether there are pixel differences in the bitmap by comparing **hex color codes**. If any color code differences are identified, then a snapshot bug is reported or an image showing visual differences is generated.

Snapshot testing is a significantly quicker way to identify bugs in user interfaces compared to manual testing. Snapshot testing is the preferred way of testing web applications if the application is somewhat static in nature and does not have a lot of dynamic content changes in the user interface. Snapshot testing does not handle dynamic content properly as the algorithm detects any change in content as a visual difference due to pixel changes. With all visual changes being identified as a visual difference or a potential bug, it would be impossible to have consistent snapshot images of pages that contain dynamic data.

Visual AI testing

Visual AI testing is the new generation of automated visual testing and makes use of **AI** (**AI**). The main goal of visual AI testing is to improve on the shortcomings of snapshot testing, such as handling dynamic content when testing applications. By using computer vision, visual AI algorithms can identify images and areas where our tests can run and even in the event of dynamic content, they can identify the regions where our content is allowed to be dynamic and the regions that should remain unchanged.

Visual AI testing also makes it easier for developers and testers to perform cross-browser testing. With cross-browser applications, the user can write a single test that can then be run in different **viewports** that are supported by the application. **Viewport testing** is a handy tool as it removes the burden of the developer – or the tester writing snapshot tests for every device – checking every viewport to verify that there are no visual changes.

Recap – visual testing

In this section, we learned about what visual testing is, the different types of visual testing, and when to use each type of visual testing. We learned the difference between automated visual testing and manual visual testing, and we also learned about the different types of automated visual testing. We then learned why visual testing is a preferred approach to manual testing and why there is a new generation of visual testing that improves on the shortcomings that were present in the first-generation visual testing tools. Now that we know all about visual testing, in the next section, we will explore more areas that require visual testing by understanding what viewports are and how to test them.

Understanding viewports

A viewport is the visible area of a user's web page. Therefore, the term viewport is used to measure the rectangular viewing region on a user's device. When computers were first invented, there were only a few available viewports, though that has significantly increased due to more devices being created. At the time of writing, new viewports are being created by devices such as folding phones or flipping screens, and smart televisions with different dimensions, so it is up to developers to ensure that their applications are compatible with the user's devices. With different viewports, new challenges arise in terms of making applications compatible with such viewports, and this is even a greater nightmare for testers as it is practically not possible to test an application through every available viewport.

In this section, we will explore the importance of viewports, how to approach testing in different viewports, and the role of viewports in visual testing.

Viewports and testing

Viewports play a major role when it comes to testing web applications as they show how the actual users will view the web application that is under test. At the time of writing, mobile viewports are the most commonly used viewports. This is because phones have been evolving to become the most powerful pieces of technology that are both portable and handheld. To provide good experiences for users, viewport testing should be a top priority. With viewport testing, we can check for qualities such as how responsive the web application is to different screen sizes.

Developing responsive web applications provides an advantage over non-responsive web applications as they take less time and resources to develop compared to standalone mobile applications, which are either on iOS or Android and performing the same functions.

All modern browsers allow us check and test for responsiveness when building applications. The following screenshot shows an iPhone 6 viewport rendered on a Chrome browser showing how the Cypress documentation page would appear on a mobile phone:

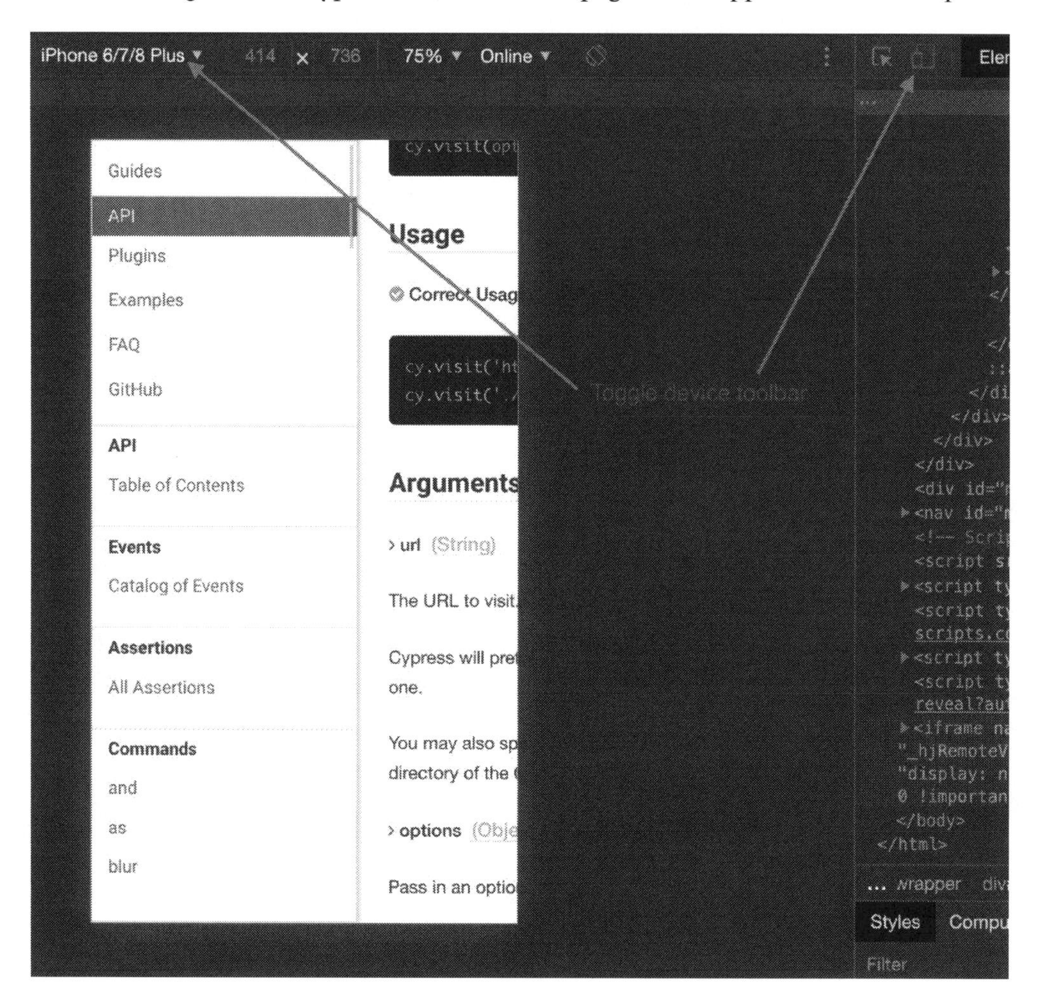

Figure 12.2 – iPhone 6 mobile viewport

We can use the **toggle device toolbar** on the browser to toggle between the normal web view and the mobile device view. This allows us to see how different web applications are rendered on different viewports. In instances where the web applications are responsive, there will be no issue testing the different viewports as the applications will automatically adapt to the changing viewports. However, this is not the case for non-responsive web applications. In the following screenshot, you can see the options for the current viewports, as well as the ability to add custom viewports that have not been defined by the browser:

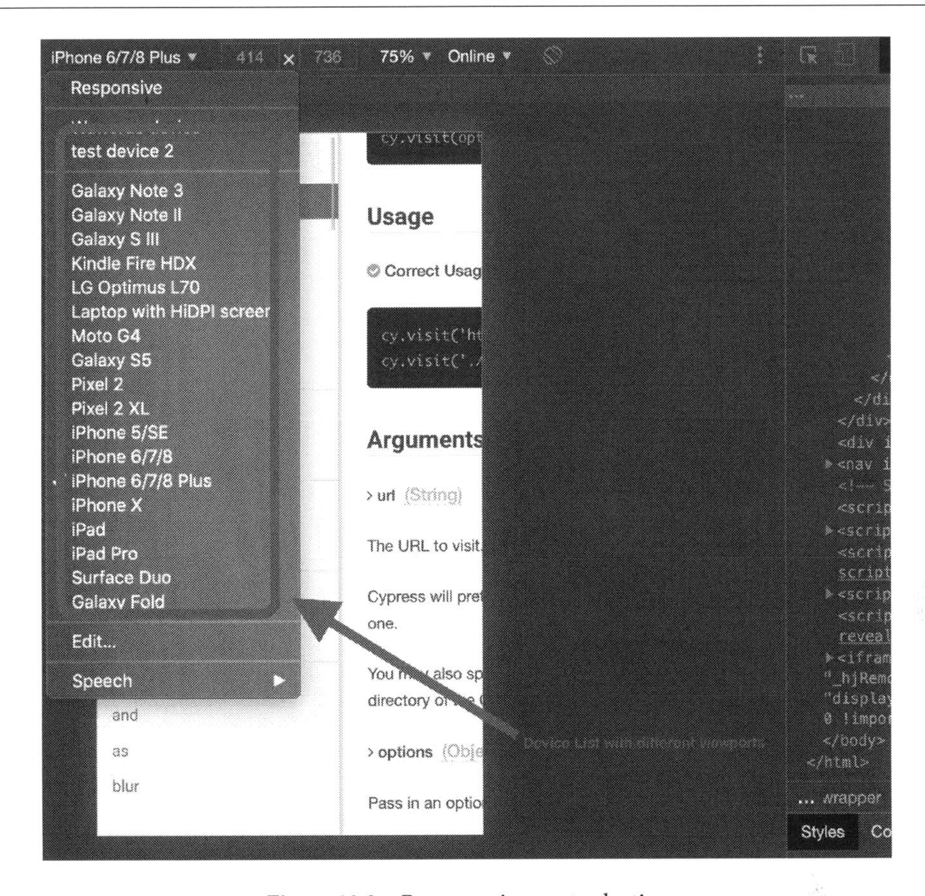

Figure 12.3 – Browser viewport selection

As shown in the preceding screenshot, it is possible to add new test viewports that do not exist in the Chrome browser's list of devices.

When choosing a viewport, the Chrome web area automatically adjusts the content that's visible on the browser. As a developer or a tester, it is easy to find out whether changes are required for the application.

Viewports and automated visual testing

Considering the number of viewports shown in the preceding screenshot, it is cumbersome to manually test every single viewport and verify that there were no changes that broke the user interface of the application, or any that introduced unnecessary changes that were not intended. To ensure that the viewports are tested, we can use automated visual testing to check for consistency in the application through different viewports. With visual testing, we can validate that no unintended changes were made to our application in the different viewports that we configure in our tests.

Recap – viewports

Viewports are a critical aspect of visual testing, especially since most of the major issues regarding web applications responsiveness are a result of viewport bugs. In this section, we learned about different types of viewports and how we can check the responsiveness of our web applications using the browser's toggle option, which switches between different device viewports and the normal computer viewport. We also learned that by using automated visual testing, we can automate different test cases for different viewports and automatically know whether unintended changes were made to the application. In the next section, we will explore how we can use Cypress to write automated visual tests using an automated Visual AI tool and Percy, which utilizes snapshots to record visual tests.

Automated visual testing tools

Visual testing is an important part of Cypress as it is a transition from what we are familiar with, which is functional testing. With visual testing, Cypress presents a new world of opportunities regarding how we can test user interfaces without necessarily writing hundreds of lines of functional code to assert individual elements on a page.

In this section, we will dive into working with two automated visual testing tools by integrating them with Cypress, and then learn how we can achieve our goals of visually testing applications using them. One of these tools uses snapshots that record a **baseline bitmap** and compare the bitmap image pixels one after the other, checking for whether there are any discrepancies in the hex colors. The other tool uses AI algorithms to compare snapshots from our web application.

By the end of this section, we will have an idea of what tool to use, when and how Cypress plays a role in creating simple integrations of the testing tools, and the tests themselves. The two tools we will look at are Applitools Eyes SDK and Percy.

Percy

Percy is a visual testing and review platform that integrates with testing tools. This enables developers and QA engineers identify visual bugs that would otherwise have been difficult to identify and report. Percy makes visual testing a walk in the park – all you need to do is to download the Percy npm module, configure **BrowserStack**, and add Percy to your tests. Once you've done all the necessary configuration, you can copy the **TOKEN** that Percy provides, which will be used as an environment variable in your machine and is required if you wish to upload your test snapshots to the Browserstack cloud to review and identify visual differences, if any.

> **Important note**
>
> Browserstack is a visual testing and review tool, and it owns the **Percy** tool. To configure Percy, you need to configure Browserstack; all the configurations will be synced between the two platforms.

Percy mainly relies on the Firefox and Chrome browsers. To test an application, Percy runs it through a set of browsers in various viewports, and any changes that have been made to the various viewports are recorded. When the first image is recorded and saved, Percy then makes the image in your test **baseline**, and will use the image to check for any changes in the subsequent test runs for similar images before highlighting any visual differences that may have occurred.

Setting up Percy

Setting up Percy is not complicated and involves the following steps:

1. Create an account with BrowserStack (`https://www.browserstack.com/`).
2. Verify your BrowserStack email address.
3. Create an organization in the Browserstack dashboard.
4. Log into the Percy dashboard using your BrowserStack account.
5. Create a project on the Percy dashboard.
6. Configure Percy on your local project using the instructions on the Percy website (`https://docs.percy.io/docs/cypress`).
7. Add a Percy TOKEN to your local machine as an environment variable.
8. Voila! You are now ready to write your tests!

Once *steps 1 - 4* have been completed, Percy provides you with a TOKEN that you must add to your machine environment variable before executing your tests. You can visit the Percy documentation (`https://docs.percy.io/docs/cypress`) for more information on how to set up Percy using Cypress.

Once everything has been set up, we can run our first test, which will involve checking whether we can see visual differences on our login page when the content is changed. As shown in the following screenshot, we have run our test by entering a username and a password on the login page:

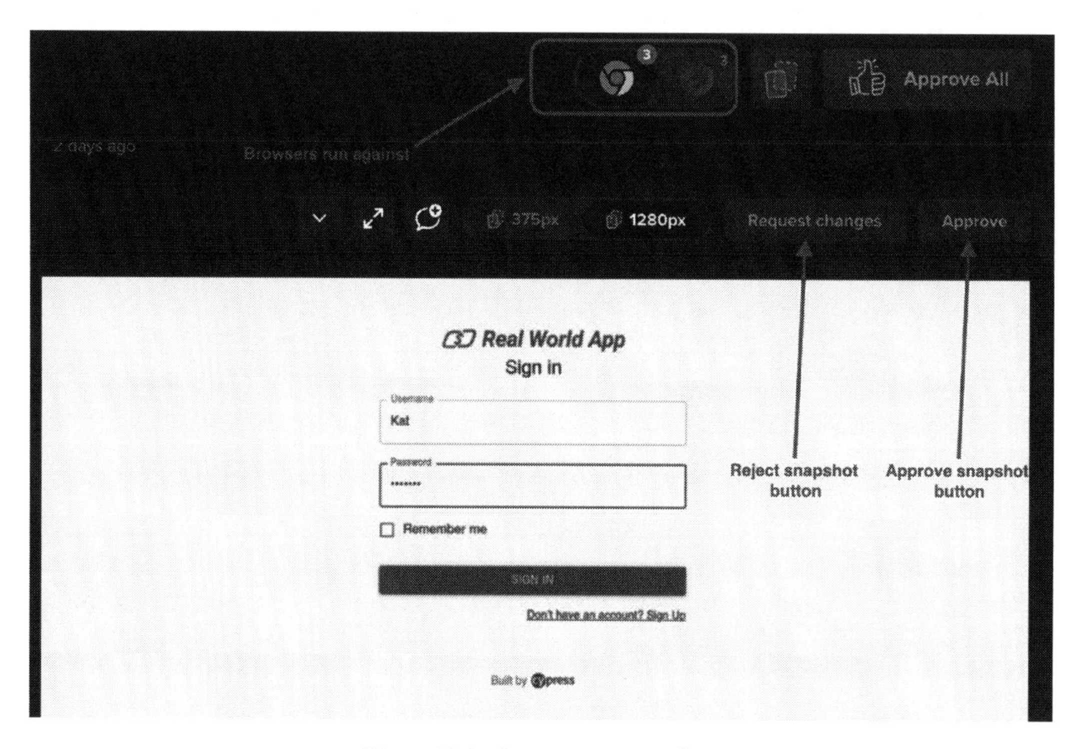

Figure 12.4 – Percy – new snapshot

Here, we can see the snapshot image that was uploaded to the Percy dashboard. The uploaded snapshot is our login page. Immediately after uploading the snapshot, Percy gives us the option to toggle the Chrome and Firebox browsers so that we can check the consistency of the snapshots. On the main Percy dashboard, we have the option to approve all our snapshots, reject and accept a single snapshot, and even toggle between the desktop viewport and the mobile viewport presented to us.

> **Important note**
>
> Percy only uploads the snapshots to the dashboard when the test's execution is terminated and the terminal running the tests is closed. This is different from the Applitools tool, which continuously uploads the test snapshots immediately when the tests have finished execution.

As we mentioned earlier, we can use Percy to compare bitmap images of our recorded baseline images and the newly generated bitmap images. The algorithm involved then checks for pixel by pixel differences, which are then recorded as visual differences when the baseline image is not similar to the newly generated image that was generated in the second run of our test application. The following screenshot shows a second build of our tests on the Percy dashboard. Here, we have omitted some of the characters in the username and password fields and we want to check whether Percy identifies these discrepancies:

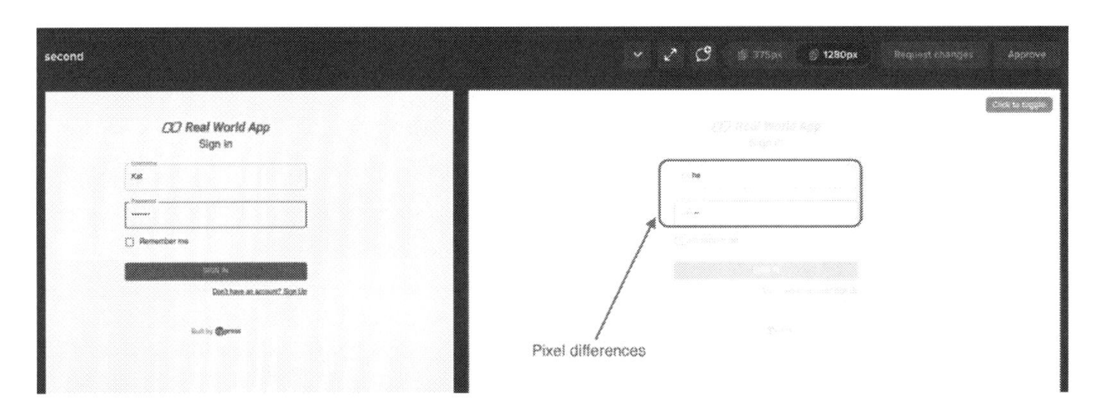

Figure 12.5 – Percy pixel differences

As shown in the preceding screenshot, once we ran our second build, we omitted some of the characters in both our username and password fields. When the snapshots are uploaded to Percy, the program identifies the visual differences by checking the pixels of the different images and provides us with the region where the pixel differences were identified. On our second run, when we *approve* these changes, Percy adopts our second image as the **baseline**. If we *Request changes* on the image, Percy will then retain our first image as the baseline for this particular snapshot.

Upon closer inspection, our first snapshot login username was *Kathe*, while in our second snapshot, the login username was *Kat*. The omission of some characters in the password and some characters in the username is what triggers Percy to show these visual differences. This gives us the option to either accept the changes and change our baseline or request changes from the developers if the change is not consistent with our expectations.

> **Reminder**
>
> For you to successfully run tests and upload the snapshots to the Percy dashboard, you need to create an account with BrowserStack, create an organization in BrowserStack, sign in with Browserstack on your Percy dashboard, create a project in Percy, and add the token provided on the Percy project dashboard to your machine's environment variables.

Percy is quick to set up, both locally on the machine and also on the tests. To invoke Percy, only a single line needs to be added to the test. The following code block shows the first and second snapshots being generated, as well as the arguments that are passed to the `cy.percySnapshot()` command for naming the snapshots:

```
describe('Percy Login Snapshots', () => {
    it('percy: signin page snapshot - first build ', () =>
      {
        cy.visit('signin');
        cy.get('#username').type('Kathe');
        cy.get('#password').type('passwor');
        cy.percySnapshot('first');
    });
    it('percy: signin page snapshot - second build, () => {
        cy.visit('signin');
        cy.get('#username').type('Kat');
        cy.get('#password').type('passd');
        cy.percySnapshot('second');
    });
});
```

The first test in the preceding code block was run in the first build, while the second test was run in the second build along with the modified username and password details to provide the pixel differences in our login page. To run these tests yourself, all you need to do is obtain the Percy token by following the Percy setup process mentioned previously and add your Percy project token as an environment variable of your machine. The complete source code for these tests can be obtained from this book's GitHub repository, in the `chapter-12` directory.

Exercise 1

In this exercise, we are going to practice what we learned in the previous section: we will learn how to use Percy to perform visual testing and then interact with the Percy configuration and dashboard. Follow these steps:

1. Using Percy and Cypress, log into our test application and navigate to the dashboard. Then, using the `Percy` command, take a snapshot of the public transactions page.
2. Add a new transaction by clicking the **New transactions** button on the application and add the transaction details.
3. Take another snapshot and use Percy to compare the transactions page's differences when another transaction is added.

> **Important note**
>
> Remember to add your Percy **TOKEN** variable, which can be obtained from the Percy project dashboard, to your local machine before running your tests so that the snapshots taken by Percy can be successfully uploaded to the Percy dashboard.

The solutions to this exercise can be found in `chapter-12/cypress/integration/percy/percy-excercise.spec.js` directory.

By going through this exercise and being able to properly set up Percy in Cypress, I believe you now understand how you can use Percy to identify visual differences in your tests, as well as quickly identify discrepancies when your application's user interfaces change. You can do this by doing a pixel-by-pixel comparison of the bitmap images of our application.

Applitools

Applitools is a tool that utilizes AI to visually test and monitor applications. Just like Percy, Applitools is easy to set up using Cypress and focuses on improving the shortcomings of tools such as Percy. Percy identifies visual differences by comparing individual pixels, while Applitools identifies visual differences by using its AI powered algorithms to check whether the changes are expected changes or bugs. With Applitools, it is easier to test dynamic changes as we can omit areas where we do not want Applitools to check for visual differences.

The ability to identify bugs by specifying regions that should be checked, and others that should be ignored, is what makes Applitools a better tool when it comes to testing applications that involve dynamic content.

Setting up Applitools

Just like Percy, the Applitools Eyes SDK is relatively easy to set up with Cypress. This can be achieved by performing the following steps:

1. Create an account with Applitools (`https://auth.applitools.com/users/register`).
2. Verify your Applitools email address.
3. Navigate to the Applitools dashboard to obtain the API key.
4. Configure Applitools on your local project.
5. Add the Applitools **APPLITOOLS_API_KEY** to your local machine as an environment variable.
6. Party!

Once *steps 1* and *2* have been completed, Applitools provides you with an **APPLITOOLS_API_KEY**, similar to the Percy **TOKEN**, that you must add as an environment variable to your machine before executing your tests. You can visit the Applitools and Cypress documentation (`https://applitools.com/tutorials/cypress.html`) to find out more about how to set up the Applitools Eyes SDK using Cypress.

Once everything has been set up, we can now run our first test using Cypress and the Applitools Eyes SDK. Applitools is a very rich tool, so we will not be able to cover all the features that it comes bundled with. Instead, we will focus on the advantages of Applitools in terms of using it as a visual testing tool. In the following screenshot, we have the same login test that we ran in our Percy example but modified for Applitools Eyes tests:

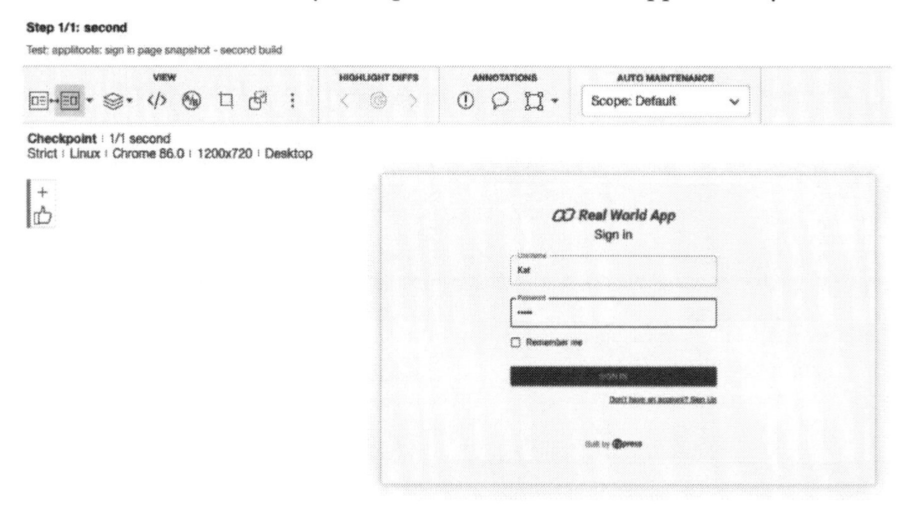

Figure 12.6 – Applitools login page snapshot

Here, we can see the snapshot representing the first login page snapshot that the Applitools Eyes SDK took and uploaded to the Applitools dashboard. Applitools uses three commands to control Cypress tests. The first command, `cy.eyesOpen()`, is for initializing and starting the test, the second command, `cy.eyesCheckWindow()`, is responsible for taking screenshots, as in the previous case, and the third command, `eyesClose()`, completes the Applitools Eyes session and uploads the screenshots to the dashboard.

Our login test can be written in the following format. This opens the Applitools Eyes SDK, takes a screenshot, and closes the SDK before uploading the screenshots to the Applitools dashboard so that they can be compared visually by the Applitools AI algorithms. The following code block shows the second build provided in the preceding screenshot:

```
it('applitools: can signin on login page - second build
snapshot', () => {
    cy.eyesOpen({
      appName: 'SignIn Page',
      browser: { width: 1200, height: 720 },
    });

    cy.get('#username').type('Kat');
    cy.get('#password').type('passd');
    cy.eyesCheckWindow('loginPage');

    cy.eyesClose();
  });
```

Here, we can observe that to run the tests, we need to initialize the Applitools Eyes SDK, then take the screenshot before closing our tests. All three methods that the Eyes SDK utilizes can have configuration parameters that can be changed, depending on your needs. In our code block, for example, we have configured the `cy.eyesOpen()` command so that we have our test batch name and the configuration of the browser window visible.

Applitools goes a step further when it comes to reporting errors. In Percy, we identified that due to its pixel-by-pixel comparisons, any change in the user interface is detected as a visual difference and potentially a user interface bug. In the following screenshot, we can see how, after running a similar test with different user interface renderings, we can tell Applitools to ignore certain regions in our screens and mark our test as passed:

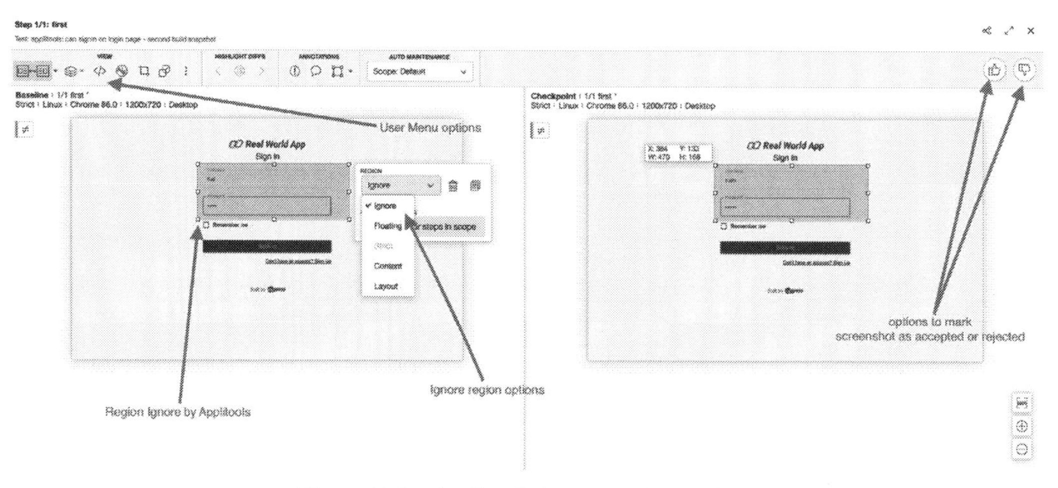

Figure 12.7 – Applitools ignore region options

Here, we can see the different options that Applitools provides. Even when different regions have different visual elements, it is possible to ignore such regions if they are not visual bugs or if they have been generated from dynamic content. After ignoring the region with visual differences, we proceeded to mark the screenshot as accepted.

> **Important note**
>
> Remember to add your **APPLITOOLS_API_KEY** variable, which was obtained from the Applitools dashboard, to your local machine as an environment variable before running your tests. This token ensures that the snapshots taken by the Applitools Eyes SDK are successfully uploaded to your Applitools dashboard.

The following screenshot shows Cypress rerunning the test and now passing it locally. It's doing this because we have instructed the Applitools Eyes SDK to accept the visual changes present compared to our baseline snapshot:

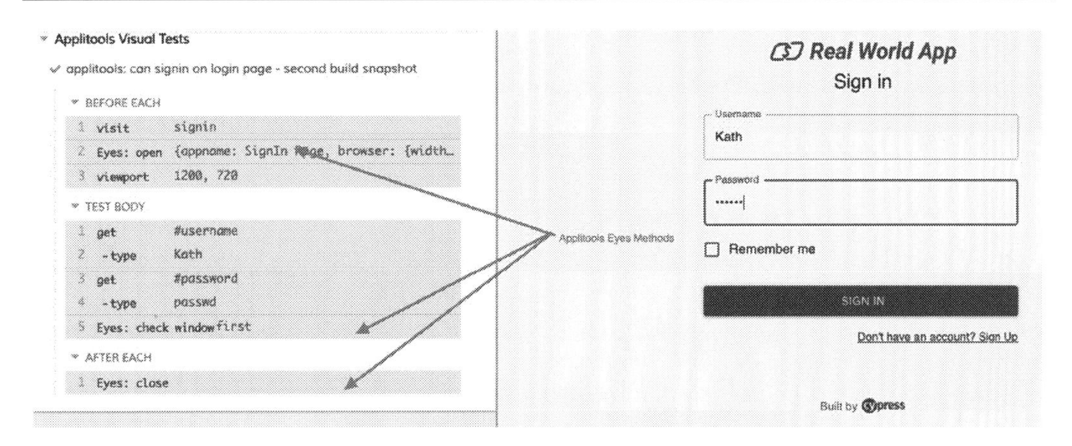

Figure 12.8 – Passing the test after ignoring the test regions in the Applitools dashboard

Voila – our test passed! Any changes that are made to the Applitools test dashboard are reflected on the local test runs. This is made possible by the API key that you must add to your environment variables before running your Applitools visual tests. You can read more about Applitools Eyes (`https://applitools.com/tutorials/cypress.html`) to learn more about how to use Applitools to test user interfaces on the dynamic modern web.

Exercise 2

In this exercise, we will test our knowledge of the Applitools Eyes SDK tool and how we can use it to perform visual testing. This exercise will help us practically implement the theoretical section of this chapter, and also find out how to use Cypress and Applitools to write visual tests. Perform the following steps:

1. Using Applitools and Cypress, log into our test application and navigate to the dashboard. Then, using `Applitools Eyes SDK` snapshot command, take a snapshot of the public transactions page.
2. Add another new transaction by clicking the new transactions button on the application and add the transaction details.
3. Take another snapshot and use Applitools to compare the transactions page differences from when the new transaction was created.
4. Ignore the region in the Applitools dashboard where the new transactions are created and rerun the test with the ignore region.

The solutions to the preceding exercise can be found in the `chapter-12/cypress/integration/applitools/applitools-excercise.spec.js` directory.

With that, I believe that you have learned how to use Applitools' automated visual testing and that this exercise has helped you harness your skills and knowledge of automated visual testing using Cypress. With that, we have come to the end of this book and by the power vested in me, I declare you a qualified "bug hunter!"

Recap - automated visual testing tools

In this section, we learned about two automated visual testing tools, Percy and Applitools, and how they can be integrated with Cypress tests. We then learned the differences between Percy and Applitools and how Percy, using the snapshot way of testing, is different from Applitools, which uses AI to analyze visual differences in tests. Finally, we learned where we can utilize testing by using tools such as Applitools. We did this by understanding how the content on browsers has changed with time and how more dynamic websites are demanding tools that can "adapt" to the dynamic content on the modern web.

Summary

In this chapter, we set out to understand how to do visual testing and its importance, as well as the viewports and tools we can use to carry out automated visual testing. Throughout this chapter, we've learned how to properly carry out visual testing. This involved understanding how to create viewports, how to test on different viewports, and also why we need automated visual tests to run on multiple viewports. We then explored two testing tools, Percy and the Applitools Eyes SDK, and extensively covered their use cases, their setup processes, and how to write Cypress tests using them. Finally, we worked on some exercises to improve our familiarity and interaction with these tools.

With that, we have come to the end of this book. If you have been consistently reading all the chapters in this book, I am confident that you have more Cypress knowledge than you started out with. I hope that this book has challenged the way you think, made you develop a love for Cypress as a testing tool, and also changed you in terms of becoming a better tester or developer.

Other Books You May Enjoy

If you enjoyed this book, you may be interested in these other books by Packt:

Modern Web Testing with TestCafe

Dmytro Shpakovskyi

ISBN: 978-1-80020-095-1

- Understand the basic concepts of TestCafe and how it differs from classic Selenium
- Find out how to set up a TestCafe test environment
- Run TestCafe with command-line settings
- Verify and execute TestCafe code in the browser
- Automate end-to-end testing with TestCafe using expert techniques
- Discover best practices in TestCafe development and learn about the future roadmap of TestCafe

Mastering React Test-Driven Development

Daniel Irvine

ISBN: 978-1-78913-341-7

- Build test-driven applications using React 16.9+ and Jest
- Build complete web applications using a variety of HTML input elements
- Understand the different types of test double and when to apply them
- Test-drive the Integration of libraries such as React Router, Redux, and Relay (GraphQL)
- Learn when to be pragmatic and how to apply TDD shortcuts
- Test-drive interaction with browser APIs including fetch and WebSockets
- Use Cucumber.js and Puppeteer to build BDD-style acceptance tests for your applications
- Build and test async Redux code using redux-saga and expect-redux

Packt is searching for authors like you

If you're interested in becoming an author for Packt, please visit authors.packtpub.com and apply today. We have worked with thousands of developers and tech professionals, just like you, to help them share their insight with the global tech community. You can make a general application, apply for a specific hot topic that we are recruiting an author for, or submit your own idea.

Leave a review - let other readers know what you think

Please share your thoughts on this book with others by leaving a review on the site that you bought it from. If you purchased the book from Amazon, please leave us an honest review on this book's Amazon page. This is vital so that other potential readers can see and use your unbiased opinion to make purchasing decisions, we can understand what our customers think about our products, and our authors can see your feedback on the title that they have worked with Packt to create. It will only take a few minutes of your time, but is valuable to other potential customers, our authors, and Packt. Thank you!

Index

D

E

F

G

H

I

L

M

N

U

V

X

Y

Printed in Great Britain
by Amazon